Robert Threlfall

SERGEI RACHMANINOFF

His Life and Music

BOOSEY & HAWKES
MUSIC PUBLISHERS LIMITED
LONDON
1973

ISBN 0-85162-009-4
Library of Congress Catalog Card No. 73-75925

PRINTED IN ENGLAND
by
Lewis Reprints Ltd.,
member of Brown Knight & Tuscott Group
London and Tonbridge.

ILLUSTRATIONS

MUSICAL EXCERPTS IN THE TEXT

*Reproduced by kind permission of Anton J. Benjamin —
Richard Schauer, Music Publishers, London/Hamburg.*

CONTENTS

INTRODUCTION

"Music is enough for a whole lifetime," Rachmaninoff once said to an interviewer, "but a lifetime is not enough for music." On another occasion, he said that he was 85 per cent musician and only 15 per cent man. When it is remembered that for the 25 years following his graduation he was known chiefly as a composer, although also as a most gifted interpreter of his own works at the keyboard and with the baton, while during the subsequent 25 years principally as a concert pianist of a fame and distinction shared with hardly any of his contemporaries, the truth of these two characteristic phrases will easily be realized. Only Liszt among his predecessors comes readily to mind; yet the travelling and concert-giving such as Rachmaninoff was still undertaking in his seventieth year were abandoned by Liszt when he was hardly more than half that age. No apology, then, is needed here for treating life and music in one continuous narrative; for in this way the pattern of the whole will become clear, as also the manner in which the one affected course and content of the other. If this account falls into three sections, these are not to be equated with the three periods so beloved of musical biographers: in the present case, the first period will deal with early days and Rachmaninoff's time as a student. Next, the first half of his professional career, covering the production of most of his mature compositions and performances of them as pianist and conductor will be examined; after which the study of his second self in his life as an international pianist will be undertaken.

At times during his life and, more predictably, in the period immediately following his death, the true value of Rachmaninoff's music was questioned by some who maybe begrudged him the extraordinary success he almost accidentally achieved at the outset of his career; and over-familiarity with some of his output — but that not entirely the less valuable part — and neglect of much of the rest made it difficult to view the whole in perspective. The early demise predicted by such critics for his more popular compositions once his own Midas touch ceased has signally failed to materialize. On the other hand, increasing interest in the less-known items of his output coupled with the scholarly issue of most of his compositions from his native land, backed by authentic performance, has led to a re-valuation of his work as a whole by a later generation no longer influenced directly by the composer's own personality, the fashions of earlier days, or the disproportionate success of one short piano piece written at the start of his career by this least publicity-seeking of public performers of his day.

In the following narrative, the first cardinal date will be given in the appropriate "double" form. All subsequent dates previous to 1918 will follow the convention of using the Old Style for events in Russia and the New Style for those taking place elsewhere. Likewise, no attempt to trans-literate Russian names completely consistently has been made; in particular, names familiar to English readers in certain forms, usually those used there by the persons concerned, are thus presented here.

THE STUDENT

Sergei Vasilyevich Rachmaninoff was born on March 20/April 2, 1873, at Oneg, near Novgorod (Gorky) in Russia; the second son of the six children born to Vasili Arkadyevich Rachmaninoff and Lubov Petrovna Butakova. Both his father and his paternal grandfather Arkadi were amateur pianists to a degree and of an application far above the average — the grandfather had indeed been a pupil of John Field — although both had originally embarked upon a career in the army. It was however the influence of his mother and his maternal grandmother that guided Sergei's doubtless hereditary gifts on their first tentative steps, for reasons which will soon become evident.

The estate of Oneg was one of five brought by Lubov Petrovna to Vasili Arkadyevich at the time of their marriage: unfortunately, her husband's unstable nature, spendthrift and improvident as it was, caused him to run through these rich possessions until, at the time of the birth of his second son, only Oneg still remained in the family. Worse was to come, for by 1882 this too had to be auctioned and the now impoverished household moved to a none-too-large flat in St. Petersburg, the nine-year-old Sergei staying nearby for a while with the family of one of his aunts, his father's sister Maria Arkadyevna (Trubnikova). Tragedy soon struck the family in the wake of a diphtheria epidemic: Sergei and his elder brother Vladimir recovered, but Sophia, their second eldest sister, died. Meanwhile the tension between the parents, consequent partly on fundamental differences but now accentuated by the gradual descent of the family from ease to near-poverty, led to a final complete break between them: Vasili left family and city and never saw his wife again.

Sergei's musical interests had first appeared in the late

'seventies while still living at Oneg, and a teacher from St. Petersburg was engaged to guide him — Anna Ornatskaya, a pupil of Cross at the Conservatoire there. After the family moved to St. Petersburg, he was enrolled as a student at the Conservatoire with a scholarship that provided for his eventual study under the same master; a plan which never came to fruition. As a boy, he took pleasure in most of the healthy activities practised by boys through the ages: he enjoyed skating, swimming, jumping on and off moving vehicles and avoiding as much organized work as possible. He early showed facility at the keyboard, and possessed absolute pitch; these gifts enabled him to scramble through his term-end examinations although in general subjects his reports were abysmally bad. By now, his father had left the family home, and an increasing influence, both personal and musical, was the presence there at intervals of Sergei's grandmother Butakova, whom he often accompanied to the Orthodox church services, thereby laying a foundation for a lifelong love of choral singing and the sound of the church bells. Mme. Butakova "spoilt" her favourite grandson, and gave him summer vacations on a farm she had bought at Borisovo, near Novgorod, no small consolation for the vanished joys of Oneg. Another increasing influence was the developing musicianship of the eldest sister Helena, who possessed a natural contralto voice of rare beauty and introduced Sergei to the music of Tchaikovsky by permitting him to accompany her in some of that master's songs. This pleasure too was destined to be of short duration; for in 1885 Helena, who had already been successfully auditioned to join the Bolshoi Opera, died in Voronezh of pernicious anaemia on the very threshold of undoubted musical fame.

By now, Sergei's erratic upbringing and spasmodic application had threatened him with expulsion from the Conservatoire; and his mother, at last clearly realizing the position, took the step which laid the foundation of all his future career. She consulted Alexander Siloti, the son of another of Vasili Rachmaninoff's sisters and himself a pianist who had just returned in triumph from a period as a pupil of Liszt himself. Siloti, after witnessing his young cousin's musical gifts and hearing of the difficulties outlined by his mother, pronounced his opinion without hesitation: Sergei should go at once to Moscow and study with Nikolai Zverev, who was a pupil of Dubuque and Henselt and had been Siloti's own previous teacher, at the Conservatoire there. Thus was the decision taken almost by chance under which Sergei became a "Moscow musician" despite his early years in the northern capital, exchanging the more receptive attitude towards innovation which then and later flourished at the St. Petersburg Conservatoire for the more conservative tradition of the old capital whose musical god was Tchaikovsky.

Zverev, it is true, was a piano professor at the Moscow Conservatoire (where Taneyev was then Principal); but it was more than just another pupil of his that the young Rachmaninoff became. It was Zverev's custom that a few exceptionally-gifted pupils, and those blessed with less of this world's goods, should lodge free in his own household, which was run on severe lines by his sister Anna, and submit to his discipline in all respects. In addition to the lessons (at the Conservatoire) and practice (watched over by Zverev's sister) there were frequent visits to concerts, opera, ballet and plays. Above all, at his famous Sunday evening parties visitors often of the eminence of Tchaikovsky and Anton Rubinstein and all the then stars of Moscow musical life were regularly welcome, and to them Zverev's young pupils played the piano. Years afterwards Rachmaninoff recalled the stimulation it was to have been brought up in these surroundings, and the encouragement it had been to perform before such audiences.

For the first year, only the piano was studied; though four-hand duet playing of chamber music and orchestral classics broadened the knowledge of these spheres, in those

9

pre-gramophone days. The climax came in 1886, when Anton Rubinstein's famous "historical recitals" took place in Moscow and St. Petersburg. Repeated for students the following mornings, Zverev and his boarders thus attended Rubinstein's unforgettable recitals twice each; and the effect on the 13-year-old Rachmaninoff could only be compared with the effect he in turn was to make in years to come on those of such an age, when memory retains every detail and the achievement of the whole world lies open and apparently possible. In May 1886 Zverev took his private pupils with him to the Crimea, where they were given an intensive course of harmony and general theory by Ladukhin, also a Conservatoire professor, in readiness for joining the harmony class of Anton Arensky in the autumn. It was probably during a similar visit the following year that, as one of his fellow students, Matvei Pressman, recalls, Rachmaninoff's first essay in composition was made. Said by his first biographer to be a "Study in F sharp" it does not appear to have survived as such; however the first of the four piano pieces originally destined to be "opus 1" is a Romance in F sharp (minor), the same key as that of the now "official" opus 1: the First Concerto. Another and earlier effort was an arrangement for piano duet of Tchaikovsky's recently-published *Manfred* Symphony, played to the composer by Rachmaninoff and Pressman at Zverev's towards the end of 1886; thus cementing the friendship with his, and Moscow's, musical idol. Rachmaninoff's first orchestral composition, a Scherzo in D minor (not F major, as sometimes stated) hopefully headed "Second Part" in the manuscript, is dated February 5-21, 1887. This fluent and brilliant little piece is obviously modelled on Mendelssohn's Scherzo from the "Midsummer Night's Dream" music, from which at least the youthful composer learnt the importance of giving a chance to his second violins. The four piano pieces intended to be "opus 1" were followed by three Nocturnes at the turn of the

10

year. All these works are now published (by the Russian State Publishers), but it would of course require more than the eye of faith to discern other than promise therein. Perhaps only the Prelude from the four pieces (in a key of later significance — E flat minor) really merits a second glance.

At Easter 1888 another meeting to have great consequences in his future took place: Rachmaninoff visited his aunt Varvara Arkadyevna (Satina), another of his father's sisters, and her children, his cousins; the second of whom — Natalia — was to become his wife fourteen years later and his inseparable companion thereafter. At the same time, he entered the advanced piano classes of his cousin Alexander Siloti, at the instance of Zverev (Siloti's own previous teacher), though Rachmaninoff would have preferred at that time to accompany his fellow-student Pressman to the class of Safonov, who was shortly to replace Taneyev as director of the Conservatoire. In view of his evident gifts for composition, as witnessed by both Arensky and Tchaikovsky, he was also to study counterpoint with Taneyev. He still continued living in Zverev's house, although the latter's supervision was now of a more general nature, the only composition of this period being some sketches for an opera *Esmeralda* which still survive in manuscript.

By the summer of 1889, however, perspectives had changed. Continued study at the raw materials of composition was about to release a mass of energy in this sphere. Two obstacles had to be overcome: Zverev's opinion that composition was a waste of so gifted a pianist, and the more practical one that in Zverev's house there was only one music-room, almost certain to be occupied by an industrious piano-practiser whenever the would-be composer wanted it for himself and his ideas. The inevitable conflict of temperaments between the adolescent Rachmaninoff and the dictatorial Zverev came to a head at this

11

time, whether for these only or for other reasons as well is now uncertain; and after an uneasy month without reconciliation, Rachmaninoff left Zverev's house and lodged temporarily with a fellow student, Mikhail Slonov, earning a frugal living from such piano lessons as he could give. From this predicament he was shortly rescued by his aunt Varvara (Satina) who gave him a room of his own and took him into the family with her own children, his four cousins. Back in St. Petersburg, meanwhile, his mother had suggested he should return there, transferring his studies to Anton Rubinstein and Rimsky-Korsakov. That to refuse such a choice was not an easy decision, one could well believe! However, it was Rachmaninoff's verdict to stay in Moscow, living with the Satin family and continuing with his studies at the Conservatoire uninterrupted, where work with Arensky (and Taneyev) on fugal composition was now added to the curriculum.

Compositions now began to flow: part of a string quartet was sketched, the first songs were composed in early 1890 and a six-part motet qualified its author to enter the fugue class. This summer was the first of many to be spent in happy surroundings at Ivanovka, the Satin family's estate near Tambov, where they were joined by the Silotis and also another family of cousins, the three sisters Skalon. Very different as the steppes around Ivanovka were from the northern forest of Oneg or Borisovo near Novgorod, let alone the more recently-experienced scenery of the Crimea, their more subtle beauty and wonder gradually exerted increasing fascination over Rachmaninoff, just as the Hungarian *puszta* was to influence Bartók in turn. Here, further music was written: another song, later to be revised as "In the silent night", op. 4 no. 3, a cello-and-piano Romance, and a six-hand valse for the three Skalon girls. More profitable, because commissioned, were the piano duet arrangements of ballet and suite from Tchaikovsky's "Sleeping Beauty" (though careful revision with Siloti's

12

help was needed to satisfy their composer before publication in the following year).

After the vacation, return to another year's work at the Conservatoire followed. A composition based on *Manfred* was commenced, but apparently left unfinished and subsequently lost; and around Christmas a visit to his mother in St. Petersburg gave Rachmaninoff a welcome break, including as it also did visits to the Skalon sisters and the chance to hear Tchaikovsky's new opera *The Queen of Spades*. 1891 began with two more musical events: the writing of a Russian Rhapsody for two pianos, and the young composer's first experience as a conductor directing his motet of the previous year. But the most important work yet was now undertaken: the First Piano Concerto, op. 1, in F sharp minor, which was commenced by March of this year and whose scoring was completed in July during another summer holiday at Ivanovka; when another song was written (op. 4 no. 2 — no. 1 followed early the next year), also a piano prelude in F later reworked for piano and cello (op. 2 no. 1), with a piano part resembling that of the concerto's slow movement and anticipating the Melody yet to come in the op. 3 group. Another piece for the six Skalon hands, this time a Romance, is more memorable for its introduction than the rest of its matter, as we shall later see. Meanwhile, friction at the Conservatoire between Siloti and Safonov, now the principal, had led to Siloti's resignation. To prevent the need of study continuing under a new master, Rachmaninoff asked Safonov to be allowed to take his final piano examination forthwith, a year early, and this permission was willingly granted: both this, for which the test pieces were Beethoven's "Waldstein" Sonata and the first movement of Chopin's B minor sonata, and the fugal examination were passed with the highest mark.

On the journey back from Ivanovka, Rachmaninoff stayed with his paternal grandmother, where he worked on the first movement of a symphony; but a chill caught swimming just before he left there laid him low on his return to Moscow with some sort of intermittent malarial fever. The Satin family being away, he was again living with Slonov; but his illness becoming serious another mutual friend, Yuri Sakhnovsky, took him in and Siloti ensured adequate medical attention, though it was six weeks before he was even on the road to recovery. He then immediately turned to the possibility of taking his final examination in composition in the spring of 1892. Arensky, to whom he dedicated in affectionate terms rare with him an orchestral work based on A. Tolstoi's "Prince Rostislav", agreed: subject to the submission of a symphony, some recitatives, and an opera. *Prince Rostislav*, a great advance in variety of orchestral treatment on the piano concerto, is again set in the much-to-be favoured key of D minor; but in freedom of form and content is perhaps the most interesting of these youthful productions. This is much more than can be said of the one-movement "youthful" symphony, also in D minor; which after a slow introduction labours to follow Tchaikovsky's Fourth Symphony by virtue of its 12/8 and 9/8 rhythm. The vocal pieces were duly completed as well (some have even been published now) and the month of March 15 — April 15 was set for the work on the opera. Before that, new excitements and experiences in the musical sphere took place: the Russian Rhapsody was played by its author partnered by the since legendary Josef Lhévinne and, in January 1892, the first public concert to reveal Rachmaninoff's gifts both as pianist and composer took place. A recently-completed one-movement Elegiac Trio in G minor and the cello prelude were given, with Brandukov's assistance, and piano solos by Chopin, Tchaikovsky, Liszt and Tausig shared place with cello solos. More important, in early March 1892, at a Conservatoire concert conducted by Safonov, the first movement of the First Concerto was performed with the composer as soloist. This, the original version of the work, was only published in full score by the Russian State Publishers as late as 1971, when the somewhat square orchestration despite the many gifted features can at last be studied in detail. Not the least striking moment in this first movement is the elaborate solo cadenza, written in a commanding piano style that only needed minimal revision when the composer returned to the work years later. The influence of Tchaikovsky is most to be noted in the Andante; that of Grieg in parts of the finale.

Rachmaninoff's father had now settled in Moscow, and shared a flat with his son; and it was living here that the one-act opera *Aleko*, based on Pushkin's "The Gypsies", was written for the final examination. Despite a delayed start reminiscent of the problems of access to Zverev's music room, caused by his father's entertaining, Rachmaninoff completed his opera in full score in three weeks, and received the highest mark again when he played it for the examining board a fortnight later. More was to come: at their unanimous recommendation he was given the Great Gold Medal of the Conservatoire, only previously awarded to two students (one of whom was Taneyev); and Zverev, forgetting any of the unpleasant past and thinking only of the pleasant past, present and future, gave his one-time student in token of reconciliation his own gold watch which was to remain in Rachmaninoff's possession for the rest of his life. He gave further proof of his genuine concern by arranging an introduction for the young author with the publisher Gutheil, who was prepared to balance his successful catalogue of popular music with a new and promising name. Gutheil soon bought *Aleko*, which he issued in vocal score (the full score only being published by the Russian State Publishers in 1953), two cello and piano pieces (op. 2) and the songs (op. 4) followed in procession by almost all the composer's output during his lifetime.

Winner of the Great Gold Medal, "Free Artist", his

prize-winning opera purchased by a publisher and shortly afterwards to be accepted for performance at the leading theatre in the land under the sponsorship of the country's favourite composer, Sergei Rachmaninoff at this stage of his life ceased to be a student and entered the next chapter of his career now as a mature professional musician "holding the world in his hands". Still very active as a pianist, though almost always only in his own compositions, and with the baton, it is nevertheless as a Composer that he is to be viewed first and foremost for the next twenty-five years, through the course of which we shall now follow him.

THE COMPOSER

At the outset of his career, Sergei Rachmaninoff possessed many gifts of mind and body to fit him for the arduous life ahead. Confident but not headstrong, independent by nature and upbringing, experienced in adversity and the loss of those near and dear, and of considerable physical resilience: all these qualities were to be needed and well tested during the years ahead to enable him to develop his many musical gifts to their fullest extent.

During the summer of 1892, Rachmaninoff gave piano lessons to the son of his then host, Konovalov, while correcting his first proofs from Gutheil and working on the piano score of *Aleko*. Here too he was visited by his mother. Shortly after returning to Moscow, where he again stayed with Slonov, he played on September 26th 1892 at a concert at the "Electrical Exposition" which he always subsequently considered the beginning of his concert career. Besides giving the first movement of Rubinstein's D minor (fourth) concerto (whose opening must surely have recurred to him years later, when he penned the climactic cadenza of his own D minor Third Concerto) and solos by Chopin (Berceuse) and Liszt (Faust-Valse), he introduced a new composition of his own — a prelude in C sharp minor. By one of those curious, unpredictable and partly inexplicable turns of fortune this one brief work not only shortly became synonymous with his very name, but was responsible throughout the musical world for the first ripples of that increasing fame that came to surround his later career. Further concerts in Orel and Kharkov followed, at the latter of which the whole group of pieces including the Prelude and now known as op. 3 were first given. Two of the other pieces, the Melody in E and the Serenade, remained favourites of their composer, who also rewrote

17

them considerably in later years.

The mounting of *Aleko* at the Bolshoi Theatre was the principal event of the early part of 1893. The Intermezzo had been played at the graduation concert in 1892 and the dances by Safonov at another concert earlier in 1893. The premiere on April 27th was attended by the composer's father and his paternal grandmother, as well as by Tchaikovsky himself, who by word and example expressed his appreciation of and confidence in this work of his young disciple. Naturally still a work of promise rather than fulfilment, this skilful score (again based on the tonality of D minor, in which key it concludes with a funeral march) shows considerable progress both orchestrally and vocally and more variety than any composition hitherto. A work of set numbers still, it will suffice to mention here, besides the brilliant dances, the chorus (No. 7) with accompaniment for strings and horns, Aleko's cavatina (No. 10) and the Intermezzo (No. 11).

Shortly after the excitements of his opera premiere, Rachmaninoff joined Slonov for the summer at an estate at Lebedin in Kharkov, where another surge of composition took place. First, the set of six songs (Op. 4) was completed with three other numbers including the beautiful Georgian Song (dedicated to Natalia Satina) and the "Harvest of Sorrow". The Fantaisie-Tableaux (Op. 5) for two pianos, dedicated to Tchaikovsky, followed; wherein the dedicatee's influence is again strongly felt, especially in the second movement (despite which the "St. Petersburg circle" received the work with smiles of pleasure), but the superb piano writing makes the work still a joy for duo-pianists. After two D minor pieces for piano and violin (op. 6), the second a lively so-called "Danse Hongroise", and another motet for mixed choir then comes a symphonic poem in E, *The Crag* (op. 7), dedicated to Rimsky-Korsakov in gratitude for the latter's conducting of the "Aleko" dances. The programme of this work lies not in

18

the epigraph from Lermontov but in Chekov's story "Along the Way", to which those same words are likewise an epigraph; and the score attempts the colour and instrumental technique of its dedicatee, as we shall also note in considering the next orchestral work. Another set of six songs (op. 8) includes the fine "Soldier's Wife" and that lyrical jewel "A Dream", dedicated to the elder Skalon sister. Now, the rest of the year was to be darkened by losses. First, at the beginning of September, Zverev died suddenly. In October *Aleko* was being staged in Kiev, and while there conducting the performances, Rachmaninoff learnt of the sudden death from cholera of Tchaikovsky on the 25th of that month in St. Petersburg. The Fantaisie-Tableaux which the composer had dedicated to him was played with Pabst in November; but now, "in memory of a great artist" Rachmaninoff wrote another piano trio in D minor (op. 9), itself an imitation of Tchaikovsky's similar memorial to Nicholas Rubinstein. This piece, in one of the most difficult forms, at times lacks balance through an overweighted piano part — a fault it shares with its exemplar, but without descending to the long lines of piano unisons as often the case in that work. Written under stress of the great emotion of its composer's loss, it yet failed to satisfy his subsequently more critical scrutiny, and a partly revised edition (eliminating the Lisztian harmonium in the second movement and making some cuts) was issued about ten years later. Meanwhile, the work was first performed at an all-Rachmaninoff chamber music concert in January 1894 together with the cello pieces op. 2, songs from ops. 4 and 8 and the piano pieces ops. 3 and 10. The latter set is as a whole less distinguished than the earlier group, save perhaps for the lively Humoresque which also re-engaged its author's attention many years later and belonged to those early works for which he retained an affection.

Rachmaninoff had about this time taken a furnished apartment in a house significantly called "America" where

19

he lived alone for a while, endeavouring to pay his way with private piano lessons (and later teaching at several girls' schools) and the sale of some popular-style piano duet pieces (op. 11). After the by now usual summer vacation at Ivanovka with his various cousins, he again moved into quarters in the Satins' house (they had recently moved to larger premises) where he could share the advantages of a home with that need for solitude and freedom from interruption which composition demanded. The next work to be completed was the "Capriccio on Gypsy Themes" (op. 12) in E, an orchestral score of an attempted Rimsky-like brilliance for which no-one in recent years, least of all its author, has been found to speak a favourable word, but which must surely deserve the occasional hearing. It was Sakhnovsky who had introduced the composer to Lodyzhensky, to whom this work was dedicated; and the latter's gipsy-born wife, the beautiful Anna Alexandrovna, now became the object of an infatuation of Rachmaninoff's. An earlier song, op. 4 no. 1, had been dedicated to her: so too was to be the next work, the largest yet undertaken, the Symphony No. 1 in D minor (op. 13) which was commenced in January 1895 and finished in the August following. Based largely on traditional orthodox service chants, dedicated "to A.L.," bearing a terrible epigraph ("Vengeance is mine; I will repay" saith the Lord) and containing much more music now utterly characteristic of Rachmaninoff himself than any previous one, this work yet had the strangest fate of any in its author's output, as will shortly be seen.

At this juncture, approaches to Rachmaninoff were made from the publisher Belaieff for inclusion of his works in the programmes of the latter's Russian Symphony Concerts in St. Petersburg; and early in 1896 *The Crag* was first performed there and generally well received, the new symphony being scheduled for performance the following season. Rachmaninoff had undertaken an abortive concert tour the previous autumn with the Italian violinist Teresina

Tua, for basically economic reasons; he now accepted Belaieff's commission to make the piano-duet arrangement of Glazunov's Sixth Symphony and contented himself with smaller works until the fate of his new symphony be known. In this way, after sketching another quartet, a set of twelve songs (op. 14) was completed which, like most of his song output, shows scrupulous and economical musical language and includes another exquisite miniature "The Little Island" (dedicated to Sophia Satina) as well as the well-known "Spring Waters", whose virtuosic accompaniment is doubtless sufficient reason for its dedication to Anna Ornatskaya, his first piano teacher. Six children's choruses (op. 15) followed, then came the six Moments Musicaux for piano solo (op. 16). These last show a considerable advance on most of the earlier piano pieces; in the second one, key and texture combine with the impatient portrayal of a mood we recognise for the first time as being the complete expression of the mature Rachmaninoff.

Ex.(1) Moment Musical, op.16 No. 2, bars 1-5

A later revision of this piece (1940) is only concerned with minor details. While the first number is somewhat Chopinesque and the final one of less lasting value, no. 3 in B

21

minor is a study in that mood later perfected in the prelude
in the same key, op.32 no. 10. No. 4, both in key and
texture is of a manner now more characteristic of Medtner,
whilst in No. 5 the spirit of the composer is just discernible
through the shade of Borodin.

March 15 was the date of the premiere in 1897 of the
First Symphony, by all accounts the most fateful date in
Rachmaninoff's career as a mature composer. (By a strange
trick of fate, the corresponding date New style was to be
that of his death 46 years later). It is difficult to recon-
struct the exact cause of what happened; but it would seem
most likely that Glazunov conducted insensitively, the
natural antipathy of St. Petersburg for Moscow accentuated
the shortcomings and occasional brashness of both scoring
and composition, and the undoubted originality of much of
the work — that personal tone of voice we have already
remarked on a few lines higher — failed to make its due
effect. This originality of form, content and expression was
remarked on by César Cui, despite the characteristically
acid tone of most of his review, and also in a more balanced
judgement by Findeisen. Rachmaninoff was overwhelmed
by the failure of his work, which he had loved dearly in
creation and now judged harshly — unduly so, in all prob-
ability. Instead of being published by the loyal Gutheil, the
composer held the work back (though he made a piano-
duet arrangement in 1898) and never sanctioned another
performance. Only posthumously were Glazunov's original
parts relocated (but not Rachmaninoff's original score) and
from them the work was reconstructed, performed first
again in Russia, published there in 1947 and thus introduced to younger generations more sympathetic than its
first audience. To them, hearing the many characteristic
touches in the first movement (which look ahead to the
later symphonies), the still rather Tchaikovskyan and very
Russian scherzo, the beautiful end to the slow movement
and above all, after the violent finale, the crushing coda

with its gong strokes and Dies Irae motif so often to be used later, it could seem that here rather than in the Second Concerto is the personality of Rachmaninoff the composer first fully revealed.

As a result of the long-lasting depression which followed the First Symphony's premiere, the author became unwilling to undertake further large-scale compositions; a few concerts and piano lessons gave him very slender support while his mind turned towards the possibility of conducting, possibly as a result albeit partly unconscious of witnessing Glazunov's failure to realise the detail of his recent great orchestral score. Suddenly he was offered, and eagerly accepted, the post of second conductor in the new private opera company run by Savva Mamontov, a rich one-time railway magnate. Here, besides lesser lights both of the stage and among the scene designers, he met the man whose genius he was to recognise and admire for the rest of his life — Fedor Chaliapin. After a false start which never survived its one rehearsal, Rachmaninoff made his debut as an opera conductor in Moscow in October 1897, with *Samson et Dalila*. Passing over works by Serov and other minor composers, it was in Dargomyzhsky's *Rusalka* and works by Rimsky-Korsakov that his gifts, despite his inexperience, became evident; and the mutual respect and admiration between him and Chaliapin continued after the end of this first season while they studied *Boris Godunov* together.

These operatic surroundings inevitably turned the young composer's thoughts to the writing of a sequel to his earlier success, *Aleko*. Having already rejected Modest Tchaikovsky's scenario for *Undine* (as also had Modest's brother, for whom it was originally destined), he now turned to him with a suggestion for collaboration on a *Richard II* to be based on Shakespeare. Modest countered with plans for *Francesca da Rimini*, and these received his collaborator's enthusiastic approval: for the moment, however, they had to be shelved while Rachmaninoff and Chaliapin toured

23

south during the summer of 1898, studying and giving recitals together. At the same time Siloti, touring Europe, England and America, had everywhere had an overwhelming success with his cousin's famous prelude: as a direct result of his English performances, Rachmaninoff himself was invited by the Royal Philharmonic Society to visit London. This he did in 1899, conducting *The Crag* and playing his Elegy and C sharp minor prelude on April 19th at Queen's Hall, all with such success that he was immediately invited to return the following year with his First Concerto, a work which he now considered immature and hence promised to surpass with a Second Concerto to be composed especially for London. (The recent Russian issue of the score of the First Concerto maintains that its author *did* perform it in London at the above time and place, but the archives of the Royal Philharmonic Society and contemporary press reports do not support this claim).

At the beginning of 1899 he had already made some desultory attempts at original composition again, besides working with Chaliapin on Rimsky's *Mozart and Salieri*. Now, on his return from London, it was to witness Chaliapin's inspired rendering of *Aleko* at its premiere in St. Petersburg for the Pushkin centenary celebrations; but the only other work of this year was the song "Fate" (op. 21 no. 1) written for Chaliapin. Again, Rachmaninoff seemed sunk into a condition of despondent inactivity and excessive self-criticism, and again the Satin family helped him by introducing him to Nikolai Dahl, a neurologist and hypnotist who was also an amateur musician. By the early summer of 1900, Dr. Dahl's simple treatment was bearing heavy fruit; by the end, after touring again in the Crimea with Chaliapin and visiting Italy whilst they studied Boito's *Mefistofele* together, Rachmaninoff returned to Russia with the score of an unaccompanied choral work to Tolstoi's words, further notes for the Francesca da Rimini operatic plan and sketches for a Second Concerto (op. 18) and a

24

Second Suite for two pianos (op. 17). By the end of the year, the second and third movements of the concerto were finished and were first performed in Moscow with great réclame, despite last-minute uncertainties due to the composer's having caught cold, to the almost too great success of home-made remedies recommended in large quantities for this condition, or to the combination of the two. Rachmaninoff easily completed the concerto, which he dedicated to Dr. Dahl, the following year and played it himself the first time in Moscow with the success that has never deserted this composition (in London it was first given shortly after by Vasili Sapellnikov). In the lovely Adagio of this work, perhaps with thoughts of the Skalon sisters, the six-hand Romance written for them is quoted; but the fascinating cross-rhythm, then merely introductory, here underpins the whole movement up to the noble closing pages. Knowing as we do that the first movement was in fact composed last, it is interesting to observe how much of the material of this movement — even the opening chords — evolves from cells or motives of the finale. When the harmony of the closing ascent of the first movement is then used as a link to the commencement of the Adagio, the circle becomes complete.

It now remained to consolidate the success thus wrought out of so long a period of fluctuating fortunes. To ensure this, Rachmaninoff approached Siloti for a financial guarantee for two years: his cousin readily assented and the sum loaned was repaid within the following year. Composition proceeded without break: the Cello Sonata (op. 19) — a chamber-music version as it were of the Second Concerto — another successful prelude, that in G minor (op. 23 no. 5), a cantata "Spring" (op. 20) with baritone solo and chorus, and another set of songs, issued with "Fate" as op. 21, wherein the masterpiece is the fragile "Lilacs" (No. 5), which Rachmaninoff later twice transcribed as an almost equally lovely piano solo. "On the death of a Linnet" (No.

25

8) is another attractive number with its piano counterpoint, more subtle than that in "How fair this spot" (No. 7). The cantata tells the story of a husband whose planned murder of his faithless wife is turned to forgiveness by the coming of Spring — that season whose arrival has been of such significance to Russians all through the ages. The motif of Spring's coming, also heard later in Medtner's second violin sonata, forms the basis of a texture which, though often spring-like in its E major music is less so in the orchestral setting of this period; as that old wizard of the orchestra, Rimsky-Korsakov, so acutely remarked. The central baritone solo has one of Rachmaninoff's favourite hummed choruses as a backing; and at the close the work rises to a great climax before receding to the distance from which it began.

By now, in 1902, Rachmaninoff was engaged to his cousin Natalia Satina and on April 29th they were married in Moscow and his days as an unsettled Bohemian were at an end. For their honeymoon, a journey to Vienna and on to Venice, returning via Lucerne to Bayreuth was undertaken; at the Wagner home, operatic experiences were added to by attending performances of the *Dutchman*, the *Ring* and *Parsifal*. Returning to Russia in time for the summer holidays at Ivanovka, the couple subsequently settled in a Moscow flat in the autumn — in the same building as "America". During this period the variations on a theme of Chopin (op. 22) were composed, a work from its Bach-like first variation full of the characteristics of the composer at the time of the Second Concerto, to which it forms a solo piano parergon. By early 1903 too another nine preludes were completed, later published with the odd G minor number as op.23 and dedicated to Siloti. Of these new piano pieces the first and last (F sharp minor and G flat major) are perhaps the most memorable, although the D minor and major pair (nos. 3 and 4) and especially the triumphant B flat major (no. 2) contain all the ingredients of popularity and effectiveness. Besides playing all these new compositions in Moscow, St. Petersburg and elsewhere, the composer travelled to Vienna to give the Second Concerto there — under that same Safonov who had conducted the First Concerto at that Conservatoire concert eleven long years before, but whose opposition first to Siloti and through him to his cousin had still not diminished.

In May 1903 the Rachmaninoffs' first child was born — a daughter, Irina. The happiness this gave to the parents was somewhat marred by the series of illnesses that dogged all three members of the family during the summer at Ivanovka, with consequently an inevitable effect on the musical productivity of those months. Rachmaninoff was now deeply embroiled in a series of operatic plans. The first of these was a musical setting of Pushkin's *The Miserly Knight* (op.24) which the composer set word for word, following the examples of Dargomyzhsky ("The Stone Guest") and Rimsky ("Mozart and Salieri"), despite the failure of either of these two exemplars to achieve lasting success. He then returned to *Francesca da Rimini* (op. 25), in whose libretto considerable alterations were made, and by dint of uninterrupted concentration this too was finished by the beginning of August 1904. Meanwhile, Rachmaninoff had been signed up as conductor at the Bolshoi Theatre for a five-month stretch commencing later that year, and with Chaliapin in the cast many brilliant successes were achieved. *Rusalka*, *Eugene Onegin*, *Prince Igor* and a special anniversary revival of *A Life for the Tsar* were followed by Tchaikovsky's *Oprichnik* and *Queen of Spades*. Early in 1905 *Aleko* was revived, and Rachmaninoff first conducted *Boris Godunov*. About this time, too, he received the Glinka prize for the Second Concerto; and a performance (under Siloti) of the cantata *Spring*, in which Chaliapin was soloist, evoked much enthusiasm also. No sooner was the opera season ended than Rachmaninoff undertook the conducting of several of the Kerzin Concerts, where his

27

memorable performances not only included Tchaikovsky's Fifth Symphony but, perhaps less expectedly, works by Borodin, Balakirev and Mussorgsky. In this way his great gifts as a conductor became consolidated and apparent to all.

During the summer of 1905, the orchestration of his own two short operas took every available moment, for performance was scheduled for the coming season. Conducting the premiere of Rimsky's *Pan Voyevoda* intervened in September, however; an occasion which not only received Rimsky's approval but also considerably deepened the ever-increasing respect felt for the older composer by the younger. Meanwhile Chaliapin, for whom *The Miserly Knight* in particular had been composed, was so dilatory about learning these new roles that another soloist, young and then unknown, Georgi Baklanov, took them over successfully after careful study with the disappointed composer. Despite the undoubtedly great musical values of both scores, the poor libretto of *Francesca* and the limited appeal of the *Knight* meant that neither achieved the success, then or later, which would have crowned the composer's work in the theatre. The *Knight*, like "Billy Budd" and "From the House of the Dead", belongs to the small category of all-male operas — a fact which adds to the sombre colour of an already dark score. Set between the sinister E minor prelude and closing pages and the rhythmic E flat first and third scenes, the centrepiece is the D minor second scene for the Baron, conceived as we know for the voice of Chaliapin. For this work alone of all his published operas the composer retained a certain liking, and in its concentrated setting of Pushkin's dramatic poem it forms perhaps a not unworthy partner to the companion works by Dargomyzhsky and Rimsky-Korsakov named already. The prologue and epilogue to *Francesca*, wherein the orchestra is joined by a wordless chorus of the moaning chromaticism of the damned (stemming in part, maybe,

28

from Liszt's Dante compositions), frame two short acts. The first is fairly conventional in content, but in the second (written a few years earlier), where the lovers reading the story of Lancelot and Guinevere declare their own love, the composer's lyrical gifts take over and carry one forward. Paolo and Francesca are not the only lovers to have heard and ignored Brangane's warnings; and indeed their somewhat tentative duet looks on to the intermezzo of the Third Concerto, just as the general tone of both these operas shows an increasingly personal language despite the preceding year's work at the Bolshoi and the honeymoon pilgrimage to Bayreuth.

Now for the first time, but by no means the last, political events in the land and the world around him began to impinge on Rachmaninoff's musical career. The December uprising in 1905 and consequently unsettled conditions prevailing, perhaps especially noticeable in a large State-run concern like the Bolshoi Theatre, reflected on the musical side; and early in 1906, despite being offered the musical directorship, Rachmaninoff severed his connection with that organisation. His next step was to travel away with his family to Italy: and here in Florence, far from the alarms and excursions of day-to-day operatic production, he soon showed that his interest in the stage was by no means exhausted. For three months he exchanged correspondence with his friends in Moscow, Morozov and Slonov; and together they worked on details of a scenario and libretto to be based on Flaubert's *Salammbo* — yet at the end of this period not a note of music had been set down (except an arrangement of an Italian polka) and other problems were becoming more pressing. Offers to conduct were received from the Imperial Theatres and from two different organisations of symphony concerts (one, the Kerzin series). Some tentative negotiations were also going on regarding an American tour. Meanwhile, various illnesses of his wife and child had impaired the value of the Italian holiday, and it

29

was with relief that the family returned to Ivanovka in July 1906, where shortly afterwards the group of 15 songs (op.26) were composed and dedicated to Mr. and Mrs. Kerzin. Most of these are charmingly concentrated miniatures and many, such as "To the Children", "Christ is Risen" and "Before my window" are well known. But perhaps the essence of the composer's gifts is to be seen within the smallest compass here in the touching D minor setting of "When yesterday we met". A firm decision was now made by Rachmaninoff as he refused all offers of engagements from Russia and America and left with his family in November (1906) for Dresden, where he settled with every intention of working uninterruptedly at composition.

The beginning of 1907, in Dresden, was occupied with necessary but time-consuming musical chores: proofreading the revised issue of the Trio, op.9, and preparation of material for a concert performance of scenes from the two recent operas, directed by Siloti with Chaliapin now taking part, in Moscow. Meanwhile, three major works engaged the composer's attention: a Symphony, the second, in E minor (op.27); a piano sonata (op.28, whose basis, though undisclosed, was *Faust*); and another opera, to be based on Maeterlinck's *Monna Vanna*. Of these three assignments it was the last, commenced in great secrecy and in close collaboration with Slonov, who was again to be the librettist, which alone fully satisfied its author. Alas, that pressures of conflicting work, and copyright complications over the use of the book, caused work to slow down and come to a standstill after completion (in piano score) of the first act and some sketches for parts of the second. Although Rachmaninoff longed to return to this most cherished of his uncompleted projects, which was one of the few manuscripts that accompanied him when he left Russia and which now rests in the Library of Congress, Washington D.C., it was not to be; and thus his operatic *oeuvre* lacks that coping-stone which, had Chaliapin first

30

impersonated *The Miserly Knight*, we might otherwise have had.

Two other events, one musical — one personal, further prevented all the hours being devoted to composition: in May Rachmaninoff played his Second Concerto in Paris, where also Chaliapin took part in a performance of "Spring", during Diaghilev's first Russian Season (Rimsky-Korsakov and Scriabin also appeared there). Meanwhile, his wife and daughter had travelled to Ivanovka, where he joined them as soon as possible; and where, on June 21st (1907) his second daughter, Tatiana, was born. For the rest of the vacation, the orchestration and review of the new symphony was a sufficiently bulky task: the sonata, the largest-scale of all the composer's solo piano compositions, also required much consideration before it took its final form. (It was one of the few piano works issued with no dedication and premiered by another than the composer: Igumnov played it first at one of his recitals in 1908, and by then it had been cut and recast in both its outside movements). Inevitably rarely played, its still great length and difficulty demand power and reserves at the keyboard so far hardly shared by any other pianists with its author; also in its comparative lack of immediately-memorable melody (except perhaps the subsidiary theme in the finale) it does not court popularity. However, the close and detailed texture points onward to the summits yet to be reached in the next two works, to which it forms a piano solo counterpart; and the exquisite coda to the middle movement, when interior trills lighten the texture, looks further ahead to the best preludes of the op.32 group. All in all, it shares with that other great Faust work — Liszt's symphony — the property of combining a study of Faust with a portrait of the artist.

During the winter season of 1907-8 Rachmaninoff took part in several concert performances, of which the most important were those in Berlin and London (Second Con-

31

certo, May 26th 1908) marking the debut as a conductor of Koussevitzky, the erstwhile double-bass virtuoso and leader of that section in the Bolshoi orchestra. In January-February came the first performances of the new Symphony, in St. Petersburg and Moscow. In four movements lasting a full hour, this noble work applies the methods of the Second Concerto to a wholly orchestral score, as full as that concerto was of its composer's own musical personality which has by now outgrown its earlier influences, even that of Tchaikovsky. There are moments in the slow movement, also in the second groups of both outer movements, as lovely as any the composer ever wrote; though probably nowhere else does he reach to the level of the closing pages of the Second Concerto's Adagio. In later years he subjected the symphony to fairly extensive cuts, now (as with those in the later Third Concerto) frequently restored. Many other of his major works were similarly compressed during the period of dissatisfaction that, as with Tchaikovsky, often supervened on completion of their scores. The rest of 1908, despite a summer at Ivanovka rendered largely unproductive due to proof-reading, was chiefly devoted to further concerts in Holland and Germany. There was a moment's relaxation however in October, when a letter to Stanislavsky for the Art Theatre's anniversary, in the form of a song, was sung to great effect by Chaliapin at the celebrations in Moscow. By the end of the year, disappointment at Nikisch's withdrawal of the new symphony from some of his programmes was compensated by the award of the Glinka Prize for this work.

The year 1909 was to be one of the most significant yet for Rachmaninoff: firstly, intensive and continuous work at the beginning of the year led to the completion of a beautiful and closely worked-out tone poem based on Böcklin's picture *The Isle of the Dead* (op.29) dedicated to a new Dresden friend, N. von Struve; of which the musical texture incorporates a later favourite motif — the plainchant Dies

32

Irae. This was first introduced to a Moscow audience by its composer in April (and shortly afterwards, as with its two predecessors, it was fairly extensively revised before publication). It was also at this time that Rachmaninoff was appointed Vice-President of the Imperial Russian Music Society, which gave him special responsibilities amongst others for the conduct of the sponsored provincial music colleges in Russia, and which he exercised with characteristic integrity and thoroughness. But the two most outstanding, and linked, events of the year were the final settlement for a first American tour of 20 concerts (commencing in November) for which a new piano concerto, the third in D minor (op. 30, dedicated to Josef Hofmann), was written straight off during the summer at Ivanovka. Work on this, despite some interruptions such as those to celebrate Koussevitzky's setting-up of a publishing house for Russian composers, extended to the degree that the composer had to use a dumb keyboard on board ship, for the first and last time, to ensure familiarity with the solo part of his intricate new composition. In this work all the facets of the composer's art as revealed hitherto in varying contexts are synthesized and raised to a new height. After the magically-scored accompaniment to the characteristic opening theme, the piano part becomes a Bach-like *obbligato* (as reference to the finale of the latter's D minor harpsichord sonata will quickly reveal) of ever-increasing richness. Next the orchestral entry and short crescendo and diminuendo (see plates 2-3) set the tone and scale for a work combining the technical finish of *The Isle of the Dead* with the broader appeal of the Second Concerto. The formidable cadenza, with its woodwind soloists at one point, the rounded conclusion of the first movement with the same theme as its opening, the so-called Intermezzo — a series of improvisatory variations of great eloquence — and the finale, alternately bizarre and lyrical, ending with the apotheosis of its lyrical element in a noble conclusion: all

33

these combine to form a work of considerable fascination as of endless technical interest, and of great pianistic effectiveness despite its notorious difficulty. In later years, perhaps originally to accomodate the work to the limits of "78" gramophone records, the composer sanctioned and indeed himself performed a cut version of the second and third movements. From the Intermezzo a mere episode was excised; but the cuts in the finale unbalanced the structure and dynamic sequence of the work, and these concessions are now best ignored by all serious pianists who tackle the concerto.

Just as this fine work sums up and transcends all its author's earlier compositions, the American tour which started in November and finished in February 1910 was the epitome of Rachmaninoff's concert life of the previous decade and more. Among the 20 appearances as recitalist, composer and conductor, pride of place must go the premiere of the Third Concerto in New York on November 28th under Damrosch and its subsequent repeat in the following January under Gustav Mahler. The Second Symphony and the "Isle" were conducted by the composer, who also gave recital programmes including the Sonata and (on one occasion) accompanied some of his songs. Despite the strain of concentrated "concertizing" on this scale, the artistic success of the whole venture was so assured that Rachmaninoff was invited to accept the post as conductor of the Boston Symphony Orchestra, or at any rate to return the following year for a further tour. To these offers he turned a deaf ear, and it was international rather than wholly personal decisions that ultimately led to his return to the U.S.A., and that not for another ten years.

Back in Russia, where the new concerto was first played (not without delays due to the wanderings astray of the material) in April 1910, Rachmaninoff became now the owner of the much-loved Ivanovka estate, over which he had had partial responsibility for some time. For the re-

34

maining years until political changes forced him to leave Russia, Ivanovka was not only a place for rest, relaxation and (hopefully) composition, but also a centre of interest for his skill in management and development of the estate, into which most of his earnings were now reinvested. Behind the more familiar picture of the reserved concert artist, we can only with some difficulty imagine the composer following the plough, directing the planting of his crops and effortlessly riding his beloved horses. This first summer with this new outlook, however, still gave birth to two very different works; the Liturgy (op. 31) and thirteen more piano preludes (op. 32) to complete the set of 24. Neither of these, of course, approaches the two previous opus for content or significance: although the Liturgy was well received (and composed "straight off", like the Third Concerto) it seems to have failed to retain interest and, as usual, the composer was in the van of its later denigrators. Various adaptations for Western use were subsequently issued, however, and the double chorus (No. 4a) and Kyrie (No. 7) are perhaps the most attractive movements. Rachmaninoff had written for chorus from his earliest days — his first appearance as a conductor in 1891 being to introduce an early motet — but still in this Liturgy a certain lack of flexibility in the handling of the voices remains, to be finally overcome five years later. The preludes (op. 32) reveal the advance in texture and technical detail over their predecessors which the Third Concerto shows over the Second, and which we have already noticed as we progressed through the various series of songs. Every pianist will have his own choice from this set (and indeed those who normally reject the composer are inclined to make an exception here); but the crescendo-diminuendo which is at the very heart of Rachmaninoff's muse is well illustrated by an excerpt from No. 9 in A major:

Ex.(2): Prelude in A major, op. 32 no. 9, bars 15-20

The grateful layout of nos. 5 in G, 11 in B and 12 in G sharp minor has been recognised in many performances by lesser hands; and while the noble no. 10 in B minor is probably the musical summit of the group, no. 13 in D flat major closes with a transfiguration of the coda to the earliest, the progenitor of them all: that in C sharp minor.

During the winter of 1910-11 several performances of the new Liturgy took place, the first under Danilin in Moscow in November being followed at the end of the season by others, including one under the composer with the Marinsky Opera chorus: these performances apparently met with the approval, at least at the time, of both himself and the critic Boris Asafiev if not of the ecclesiastical authorities. At the same time he had been appearing in Vienna, Frankfurt and Berlin in addition to a number of engagements in Russia both as pianist and conductor of his own works. Apart from a lively and popular concert arrangement of one of his father's Polkas,* it was late summer at Ivanovka before composition

*"Polka de W.R."

was resumed with nine Etudes-Tableaux (op. 33) which, though differing in content and technique from the Preludes as little as Debussy's later Preludes from his Etudes, suffered a very different fate. Three were withheld by the author, who released one (no. 4) later, recast as op. 39 no. 6. The other two only appeared posthumously, first in the Russian collected edition and American reprints therefrom and later in a reissue of the whole opus by Boosey and Hawkes in London. It can now be seen that whereas the mood of no. 5 was best crystallized later in the song op. 38 no. 4, and the opening section of no. 3 is at best a sketch which became perfected afterwards in op. 39 no. 7, the last page of this same third number was used, as a sigh of reminiscence as it were, at the close of the middle movement of the Fourth Concerto, not to be completed for many years yet. Of the first published group of six (actually nos. 1, 2, 6-9) the martial no. 1 and the lyrical nos. 2 and 8 are all attractive without equalling the E flat minor and major pair, nos. 6 and 7, great favourites of the composer and very grateful and effective for lesser hands firm enough to grasp such opportunities, while no. 9 is a tragic fragment again in C sharp minor.

During the autumn of 1911, a visit to London included not only a recital but the introduction there of the Third Concerto on 7th November at a Royal Philharmonic Society Concert, under Mengelberg. Back in Russia, a long recital tour included the new Etudes-Tableaux (as well as the later preludes) and as the year 1911 drew to a close musical events of special interest were a performance by Scriabin of his Concerto, conducted by Rachmaninoff, and a performance by Rachmaninoff of Tchaikovsky's First Concerto (conducted by Siloti).

It was in early 1912 that the young poet Marietta Shaginyan (signing herself "Re") commenced a correspondence with Rachmaninoff which elicited a series of grave, detailed and often thoughtful replies from the composer.

How prophetic was his statement "No wonder if I should, after a while, make up my mind to abandon composition altogether and become, instead, a professional pianist or a conductor..." the events of the next five years were to reveal. But meanwhile it was as critic and guardian of the composer's taste in poetry for use in his songs that "Re" brought most influence to bear on him, influence that soon bore fruit in the great set of fourteen songs (op. 34) mostly written at Ivanovka that summer. The first, Pushkin's "The Muse" was appropriately dedicated to Re, and others are memorials to Tchaikovsky and the actress Vera Kommissarzhevskaya; but all the remainder are inscribed to the singers whose voices they enshrine as at their early performances: several of course to Chaliapin; several others to the tenor Sobinov (including the exquisite "Morn of Life" and the gorgeous "What Wealth of Rapture"); a sinister dramatic scena "Dissonance" for Felia Litvin, and the last and crowning number of all (completed somewhat later), the famous *Vocalise* for the coloratura soprano Antonina Nezhdanova. Again, *mutatis mutandis* a Bach-like composition emerges here from the classical binary aria form with as it were a continuo accompaniment: so touching, if inevitably idealised, a memorial to its first interpreter is it that mere perusal of the printed lines as their counterpoint resolves towards the end cannot fail to strike emotion.

The rest of the year 1912 and its concerts was largely devoted to various activities as a conductor, until in December the whole family left Moscow and passed through Berlin and Switzerland on the way to Italy where they settled in Rome early in 1913. Here Rachmaninoff commenced the composition of one of his most elaborate, yet concise, and characteristic works which thereafter always remained his favourite: *The Bells* (op. 35), a choral symphony to Balmont's translated version of Edgar Allan Poe's famous poem, of which he had been sent the words shortly before by an anonymous admirer. The complete

38

mastery of all the resources employed as revealed in the *Isle* and the Third Concerto was here used with welcome concentration to produce what many agree with the author in naming as his masterpiece. The charming lightness of touch of the first movement, with its true tenor solo line, is immediately arresting; the equally characteristic cadences of the soprano solo in the second movement no less so. The very elaborate choral writing in the third movement, of which more will be said later, properly performed is of electrifying effect; and if the last movement returns to the key and the mood of the famous prelude, there is contrast in its middle section and consolation in the closing page that rounds the whole work off with a sense of certitude and finality removed from mere pessimism. In this comprehensive score is found the apotheosis of the bell sounds which have permeated so many of Rachmaninoff's works since the third and fourth movements of the Fantaisie-Tableaux op. 5, which itself enshrines memories of the Novgorod bells and the days of youth.

The Bells was basically composed in Rome, but the visit there was abruptly terminated when both children caught typhoid fever, and were taken by their anxious parents first to Berlin for treatment and then to Ivanovka for recuperation. Here, after their recovery, and among the conflicting interests of the running of the estate and driving many miles in a new treasure — his first motor-car — Rachmaninoff finished the orchestration of the work. He also completed at about the same time the Second Piano Sonata (op. 36). This work (to which the programme, if any, is not revealed) is slightly less extended than the first; although in difficulty, elaboration and intricate texture it is of the same family. The lyrical themes in the first two movements are, in their stepwise movement, very characteristic of the composer; that in the last movement, both in melody and harmony, rather recalls some aspects of Scriabin. A theme of falling fourths and rising thirds in the development section of the first movement is met again in the first published version of the Fourth Concerto (D flat section of last movement), as also (homage or parody?) in the lovely *Pas de deux* from Stravinsky's "Apollo". Dedicated to Pressman, a fellow-inmate at Zverev's, the sonata (an early favourite of another master of the keyboard: Vladimir Horowitz) was later drastically revised by the author, as we shall see. During the rest of 1913, a number of piano recitals of his compositions (including the new sonata) were given throughout Russia by the composer, but the musical climax of the year was the premiere of *The Bells* in St. Petersburg at the end of November, the Moscow first performance following in February 1914. Between these two concerts, a short tour in England took place, during which provisional arrangements, destined to be postponed, were made to perform *The Bells* at the Sheffield Festival later in the year. For the rest of the summer of 1914, the work at Ivanovka itself occupied its owner — this time to the utter exclusion of any musical composition — and by the time of the return to Moscow to conduct a memorial concert to Lyadov, the First World War had broken out.

At the beginning of this season, a number of charity performances were given under Koussevitzky's direction by Rachmaninoff, who also later contributed a stern page of setting from St. John's Gospel to a war relief album. Despite thoughts of writing a ballet, destined to materialise under very different circumstances a quarter of a century later, no music was written during 1914. Nevertheless, the early weeks of 1915 were blessed with the creation of another masterpiece; a rare work indeed this, on as high a level as *The Bells*, even in the critical eyes of its author, but denuded of all the orchestral and instrumental complexity of that and any earlier success. This was the Night Vigil (Vesper Service), op. 37, for unaccompanied voices. Apart from the fifth movement, preferred by the composer, which closely resembles part of the last movement of *The*

Bells, other highlights of the long work are nos. 2 and 11, the Glorias (nos. 7 and 12) and the two Hymns to the Mother of God (nos. 6 and 15); and the uncanny variety of colour and texture first revealed in no. 2 remains, once heard, as a memory never to be dimmed. Completed in a couple of weeks and at once accepted for performance by the Synodical Choir leaders, the new work was first performed in March, four further performances for war relief charities quickly following. Approval and admiration poured in from all sides, from supporters and erstwhile critics, who all stood united before this natural and beautiful creation, so far removed from the concert world of the famous piano solos and concertos, and to this day perhaps the most lofty, if lonely, height reached by its composer.

Amongst the praise for his new work in the new-old austere style, none was more valued than that from the author's old mentor, master himself of the contrapuntal muse *par excellence*, Taneyev. None too was more timely, for in June 1915 Taneyev died, of the consequences of a cold caught at the funeral of a younger master, Scriabin. To the memory of the first, Rachmaninoff wrote a dignified letter of eulogy; to that of the second he proposed a more practical tribute, in that he dedicated a series of recitals to a programme of Scriabin's works which, after playing the latter's piano concerto in St. Petersburg, he introduced in Moscow in November. At a stroke, this well-meant and generous gesture crystallized the hostility which, on the fringes of all great reputations, needs only a focus on which to concentrate. Whereas to us now, at the safe distance of over half a century, much of the music of these two pianist-composers, one-time fellow-students, falls inevitably into the same category, Scriabin had at the time of his death become (and not only for musical reasons) the prophet of futurism; and those who had blamed him as such tended to perform the not unusual somersault on his

41

death and to praise him, reserving their blame then for Rachmaninoff, who was thus denounced as a conservative and whose first extensive championship of another composer's writing was dismissed for partly personal reasons disguised as partly musical ones. If it be true, as no less an authority than Gennadi Rozhdestvensky has said, that the essence of Scriabin is as subtle as that of Beecham's Delius, it is well to recall that to Sabaneyev, that lifelong disciple of Scriabin, Rachmaninoff's performance of Scriabin's music was "in its own kind stamped with genius, like everything that pertained to Rachmaninoff's performances". Koussevitzky, in many ways the upholder of Scriabin — of whose orchestral works he was the eloquent interpreter — had already conducted one of Rachmaninoff's performances of the concerto. He now gave a special Rachmaninoff concert, including *Spring* and *The Bells*, to which the author contributed his Third Concerto; and Gutheil the publisher having died, Koussevitzky bought up the latter's firm (with almost all Rachmaninoff's copyrights hitherto) and published the Night Vigil (Vespers), the first of the composer's works to appear over the new imprint, in the same year (1915). The Vocalise was introduced by Nezhdanova, to the composer's accompaniment, at another Koussevitzky concert early in 1916.

With war in the world around them and revolution close ahead for their native land, the year 1916 however started along the pattern made familiar from many previous years: recital tours, ending with a family reunion at Ivanovka in the summer. The start of the summer this year was darkened by the death there of Vasili Rachmaninoff, visiting Ivanovka for a few weeks, during the absence of his son who was then taking a cure at Essentuki in the Caucasus. While there, the composer renewed acquaintance with the soprano Nina Koshetz, whom he had already accompanied, and they agreed to give concerts of his songs together during the next season. Composition of a group of new songs (op. 38) for inclusion in this programme proceeded at Ivanovka: eight were drafted, but two remained in sketch. The words for all those completed and published were by the more "modern" poets recommended by "Re", and so the cycle as a whole is a memorial to her choice of poems as well as to the voice of Nina Koshetz which first brought them to life in sound. The most popular of the group is "Daisies" (no. 3), which was transcribed by Kreisler as a violin solo and by the composer as a piano solo; but it is in the fifth song ("The Dream"), the last to be composed, where (as Scriabin would say) "the dream takes shape" in a lovely melody in canon between singer and accompanist, that Koshetz's voice received its memorial, the equal of Nezhdanova's in her Vocalise. At the same time, Rachmaninoff commenced the last and most ambitious of his sets of piano pieces to precede the break in his career: the Nine Etudes-Tableaux, op. 39. When these and the recent songs were heard in concerts during the ensuing season, the development for which the composer's musical language had been striving was remarked by all critics — friendly and less so — witnessing as they did the irregular barring, freer harmonic relations and chant-like melodies that pervade these pieces. Apart from the sixth (itself recast from the earlier op. 33 set) even the most passing mention must refer to the "Isle of the Dead"-like ripple of no. 2; that devilish scherzo, no. 3 in F sharp minor, one of Rachmaninoff's very best works; and the long and exceptionally difficult no. 7 in C minor. Perhaps the finest of all, maybe even the finest single short piano solo work he ever wrote, is no. 5 again in E flat minor, which together with the martial concluding no. 9 in D was not finally set in order until the following February. A passage from the middle of the E flat minor piece shows the old technique and style still at the service of ever more flexible ideas:

43

*Ex.(3): Etude-Tableau in E flat minor, op. 39
no. 5, bars 33-36*

The closing pages of this great work sink to a resigned and peaceful end in the major, after a gigantic climax wherein the opening melody returns as if from trombones, memorable indeed under the composer's mighty yet sensitive hands.

For Rachmaninoff as for all of his countrymen, 1917 was to be the fateful year. At the start, however, a concert he conducted in Moscow with *The Crag, The Isle of the Dead* and *The Bells* left no doubt of his achievement or the esteem in which he was held. After a recital tour of the south he returned to Moscow; and the very day of the Tsar's overthrow he was giving a charity recital there for the army wounded — his last recital in Russia as events determined. More charity appearances, playing the Liszt and Tchaikovsky first concertos as well as his own Second, followed after which he returned for the last time to Ivanovka; thence the family, greatly concerned about events around them, spent the summer in the Caucasus. Rachmaninoff's last concert in Russia occurred in September, when he played the Liszt concerto in Yalta. In October, returning to their Moscow flat, the composer at last took up his First

44

Concerto and, as he had long intended, completely recast it. Reissued still as op. 1 (though a Prokofiev would doubtless have more appropriately labelled so far-reaching a revision op 1/39B), the first two movements retain their original themes and general layout but the whole is now rethought by the mind that had just conceived the recent Etudes-Tableaux. The third movement, shedding its Grieg influences, and developing the characteristic treatment of the central song now in E flat instead of D (which was later to have some influence on the Andante of Shostakovich's second concerto), wisely removes the Lisztian apotheosis of that lyrical theme and substitutes a recomposed finish, effective without being too weighty. A few other musical drafts matured: the *Oriental Sketch*, only to be published and performed decades later, and the wistful *Fragments*, a "Lilacs"-like page of reminiscence, as well as an untitled D minor piece still unpublished. But by then the Revolution was taking place, and there was no more thought of composition nor conducting, concerts nor opera for Rachmaninoff in his homeland. At this very moment he received an utterly unexpected invitation to give concerts in Stockholm; and visas being obtained not only for the composer but for his whole family, they all left Russia never to return in December 1917 accompanied by their close friend from Dresden days, Nikolai Struve, and arrived in Stockholm on Christmas Eve.

At this point in time, the composer's career underwent a radical reorientation as a result of the upheaval thrust on to him by leaving Russia. No more will he be thought of first and foremost as a composer, for the successful author of the Prelude in C sharp minor now became a professional pianist, as he had once foreseen in the letter to "Re" from which we have already quoted; and it is henceforward as a concert pianist that he moved on to even wider audiences and broader fame, in a "third period" wherein his exceptional gifts at the keyboard were now primarily placed at the disposal of the music of others.

THE PIANIST

Hitherto, in this short account of the life and works of Sergei Rachmaninoff, a balance has been held between the events of the one and compositions of the other. Now that for the remainder of his years Rachmaninoff became a virtuoso pianist with his home in the United States, to avoid too disproportionate a space being given to a mere listing of a bewildering number of concert engagements, generous time will occasionally be allocated to items of more general interest. At the same time, the production of new compositions almost ceased for years on end: whereas in earlier days the summer vacations at Ivanovka witnessed the birth of most of the works — only a few exceptions, such as the Night Vigil, being written in the city during the concert season — the absence of a substitute for that place for many years, together with increasing business and social activities, explains the corresponding absence of original composition. And when a return was first made, cool critical reception caused another period of silence to intervene before the final phase of comparative productivity.

Although Rachmaninoff had left Russia to give a concert tour based on Stockholm, as a result of the upheaval the whole family had undergone this was deferred while a temporary base was first set up in Copenhagen, where a recital and a performance of the Second Concerto were given in February 1918. In March the Stockholm concerts followed, and a total of ten more concerts were given in Scandinavia by July, including the Tchaikovsky and Liszt concertos — but the recital programmes still consisted only of the composer's own works. It was at this stage that Rachmaninoff, realizing the inevitable drift of his fate towards the new career of a virtuoso pianist, for the first time since his student days commenced the study of the "miscellaneous" programmes which he offered for the rest of his life. (Curiously enough, despite the recent performances of the Tchaikovsky and Liszt concertos, almost all his future appearances with orchestras were to concentrate on his own concertos with later and very rare exceptions for Beethoven's first concerto, Liszt's "Totentanz" and the Schumann concerto, at the very end of his career). These new programmes were displayed during a series of 14 more Scandinavian concerts during September and October, and the season was clinched by a performance of the Second and Third Concertos at a final concert in Stockholm, after which the next decisive move took place.

During the year's Scandinavian interlude, no less than three major offers from America were received by Rachmaninoff: a two-year conductorship at Cincinnati: a series of 25 piano recitals: and an engagement with the Boston Symphony Orchestra to give 110 concerts in 30 weeks. Although he did not accept any of these offers, he determined to go with his whole family to America, convinced that there a new future awaited them all. The legal formalities were simplified by the concert offers received, even though they had been refused; the journey was safe and uneventful; but a crazy welcome awaited the travellers when they awoke on their first morning on American soil: it was Armistice Day 1918, being celebrated with characteristic abandon in New York. Many friends, old and new, soon gathered around the newcomers — headed by Kreisler and Josef Hofmann — and concert agents and recording companies competed for the services of the distinguished visitor. Before any practical steps could be taken, however, an attack of "Spanish 'flu" laid low the composer and his daughters, but by December 8th 1918 Rachmaninoff's first American concert as a resident took place in Providence, Rhode Island quickly followed by successful recital appearances in Boston and New York. Shortly afterwards concerts with orchestra followed, at one of which the rewritten First

Concerto had its first public performance. Among other musical highlights were a recital of piano music by Scriabin, Medtner and Rachmaninoff (Chopin Variations and Etudes—Tableaux, op. 33), a performance with Casals of the cello Sonata and (at a charity concert to end the season) a performance of Liszt's Second Hungarian Rhapsody with an elaborate cadenza by Rachmaninoff. (Apparently never committed to paper, this was post-humously reconstructed by Jan Holcman from the Edison recording, and published in 1955).

A summer holiday at Menlo Park, Palo Alto, Calif., gave welcome opportunity for the practice necessary for fresh programmes, and during the 1919—20 season many per-formances of the Third Concerto (and also of the Liszt) were given; a recital programme of Etudes by Chopin, Schumann, Rubinstein, Liszt, Scriabin and Rachmaninoff was also introduced. In February 1920, the American premiere of *The Bells* took place in Philadelphia under Stokowski; and in April a movement from the Night Vigil (no. 8), which work had just been published in America in an English edition (as "Songs of the Church") was given in New York by Damrosch. The summer vacation this year was spent nearer "home" — at Goshen, N.Y. — and a few desultory arrangements of Russian songs were made at this time. The beginning of the 1920—21 season had a shadow cast over it by the news of the death, in an accident in Paris, of Nikolai Struve. Although this season did not commence until November, in the following five months a series of 41 recitals and 13 concerto appearances (including the Tchaikovsky concerto) took place — already an indica-tion of Rachmaninoff's increasing success and popularity in his new homeland. At the conclusion of this tour, he took a New York apartment (33 Riverside Drive) and then settled for the summer holiday at Locust Point, New Jersey, in an atmosphere of relaxation to which Russian company and customs contributed not a little.

48

Plates 2-3. Third Concerto, op. 30.

Two pages (11-12) from the full score.

Plate 4: Third Concerto, op. 30. A page from the manuscript of the full score, 2nd movement.

Another "feature" programme was introduced during the 1921—22 season, this time including Ballades by Chopin, Liszt and Grieg; and a degree of Doctor of Music was given him by the University of Nebraska when the composer played there in January 1922. A number of attractive concert transcriptions for the piano date from this period despite the continued absence of original composition: Kreisler's Liebesfreud' and Liebesleid, the Minuet from Bizet's 1st Arlesienne suite (of which an arrangement made in Russia twenty years earlier was also published in the Russian collected edition) and probably the Scherzo from Mendelssohn's "Midsummer Night's Dream" music — this last and most difficult, however, not being issued until ten years or so later. After a couple of final concerts for Russian charities, Rachmaninoff sailed for the Old World, where he gave his first post-War recitals in London on May 6th and 20th 1922, being received there with the warmth which was his whenever he visited that capital. At the end of the concert season, Rachmaninoff was in Dresden again where his cousins the Satin family, now having succeeded in leaving Moscow, had also settled. Renewed personal contact with them, and the renewal too of correspondence with old friends remaining in Russia such as Wilshaw and Morozov, together with fairly regular correspondence with his mother and brother, deepened his sense of the loss of his homeland which dominated all the remainder of his life. A long series of gifts and parcels to persons and institutions remaining in Russia pay tribute to his generosity and essential, fundamental, patriotism; and his joy at meeting the members of the Moscow Art Theatre when they visited New York around this time knew no bounds.

The season 1922—3 was the busiest yet — both in number of concerts (of which there were no less than 71) and in the area covered, which now included Canada and Cuba as well as the U.S.A. A tour of Australia, which had been proposed to follow these engagements, was cancelled however. To facilitate travel and reduce the problems of accommodation and practice, Rachmaninoff lived in a specially-equipped railway observation car during this period; his letters to Wilshaw and his secretary, Somov, reveal that the keenly self-critical nature that had watched over the composer in the past was still in charge of the concert pianist: "I make some progress, but actually the more I play the more clearly do I see my inadequacies," he wrote. In a letter to Morozov, Rachmaninoff explains how rarely he thinks now of composition: only the thought of the work commenced before leaving Russia (the Fourth Concerto) spurs him on, and he hopes perhaps "this summer I'll try to get to this." Actually another two years were to pass before this took place; but meanwhile the only concert arrangement of the period was of a Russian work: Mussorgsky's Gopak. The early piano Serenade (op. 3 no. 5) was rewritten and elaborated about this time, and recorded on an Ampico roll; but this version, together with some other similar revisions, was not published until 1940. A considerable reduction in the number of concerts planned for 1923—4 was agreed: fifteen before the end of 1923 and (after a one-month gap) fifteen more early in 1924, followed by a recital at the White House. Shortly after this, the family left for Europe, spending a period in Naples and Florence and then travelling via Zurich to Dresden: during part of this holiday, time shared with Medtner was a particular pleasure. This year, the period in Dresden was lengthened, the family staying until after the wedding of Irina Rachmaninova to Prince Peter Wolkonsky which took place there in September; immediately after which Rachmaninoff crossed to England for a series of concerts (including London recitals on 6th and 16th October 1924) before returning to America, where the first recital of the season was in Boston in November.

Again, a series of appearances on similar lines was planned — and it must be remembered too that many periods of apparent "holiday" between fixtures were devoted to the making of gramophone records and player-piano rolls — lasting until April 1925: a second White House recital took place on January 16th. In his review of the season in a letter to Wilshaw written in May, Rachmaninoff was already planning ahead to have no concerts after December 1925 for a spell — and this time the plan was to bear fruit. Meanwhile, after a rest in Dresden the family settled near Paris for the remainder of the summer, where in August the sad news reached them of the death of Peter Wolkonsky just before the birth of his daughter Sophie, Rachmaninoff's much-loved grand-daughter. It was just at this time that the composer set up a publishing house in Paris under the name of Tair (a name based on his daughters' initials) primarily to issue works by Russian authors which might otherwise be doomed to silence. This house also published the later works of the composer himself in Europe, one of which — the arrangement of Schubert's "Wohin" — dates from this period and forms an interesting contrast to the Liszt arrangement of "Das Wandern" which was such a favourite encore of Rachmaninoff's.

At last, the sabbatical year was at hand; and despite inevitable interruptions of one sort and another, and passing through Paris to Dresden yet again, the Fourth Concerto (op. 40) was completed there in August 1926 and dedicated to Medtner, who was simultaneously working on his own Second Concerto which he in turn dedicated to Rachmaninoff. On receiving the copyist's score, the composer was horrified at the bulk of his new work; and with a gibe about performance being spread over three nights — like the "Ring" — set about some little-known, but substantial, cuts and alterations which intervened before publication. This new work, whose completion was so long delayed, and which was yet to receive final revision in its author's last year, inevitably reflects the subtle changes of style the composer's art had undergone during that period.

51

Without calling for either the exceptional power of the Second or the exceptional technique of the Third, the endlessly fascinating patterns of the solo part of the Fourth, wherein every note is clearly heard, deserve at least the occasional attention of pianists and their audiences in search of a work a little off the beaten track. By the end of the first movement, the characteristically soaring opening theme becomes a floating, hovering *tranquillo* in high violins, underpinned by piano arpeggios and the ever-present Dies Irae in a memorably lovely moment. The short intermezzo-like largo, which as the composer later realized resembled Schumann (but to his English audiences "Three blind mice") closes with the wistful pages transferred from the "withdrawn" Etude-Tableau, op. 33 no. 3; or rather now leads straight into the brilliant and darkly glittering finale, a movement of at times almost barbaric colour and a harmonic astringency and instrumental brilliance new in the composer's work.

On returning to America in November 1926, Rachmaninoff brought with him another new composition, one of his least-known but most attractive works: Three Russian Songs (op. 41) for chorus and orchestra, dedicated to Stokowski. In complete contrast to the earlier great choral works opp. 35 and 37, here the vocal part is of utter simplicity, often remaining in its original monodic form: the orchestral commentary in its variety and cumulative brilliance, especially in the rhythmic third song with its lovely instrumental interlude, carrying the narrative on in irresistible fashion.

Before either of these works was heard in public, the composer took up his concert career afresh, after the extra work necessitated by his year-long lack of practice, in February 1927. The following month the two new compositions were performed under Stokowski, first in Philadelphia (March 18-19) and immediately afterwards in New York. Despite a *succès d'estime* with most audiences, the

52

general critical reception of the new concerto was so indifferent that the composer soon withdrew it from further performances in America; the songs, though more attractive and successful, unfortunately shared in their brother's fate and only became firmly established years later — in Russia itself, not surprisingly. Thus Rachmaninoff's long-delayed return to composition was followed by another five-year period of complete silence, before his natural diffidence was overcome by a genuine creative stirring which on that occasion was not only better received by his audiences but also based on firmer foundations.

After the disappointing 1927 season, which Rachmaninoff nevertheless finished with a performance of the Fourth Concerto, the family left for Europe, where this year a considerable time was passed in Dresden and later in Switzerland. The 1928 American season started in January with a "feature" programme of Fantasy-sonatas — the Beethoven (Moonlight), Chopin and Liszt (Dante) — and finished in April with a charity concert for Russia, after which Rachmaninoff crossed to England for his single London recital on May 19th. The summer this year was spent on the Normandy coast with many visitors old and young, including the Medtners close by; afterwards the family moved to Dresden for the composer to commence work for a European tour planned to occupy the rest of the year 1928. Starting in Copenhagen in October, and passing through Scandinavia and Holland to reach Berlin in November, the tour became so successful as it continued through Dresden, Prague, Vienna and Budapest to finish in Paris in December that future plans were based on a similar tour sharing the months with the regular transatlantic one. Meanwhile, 1929 started with a series of 31 recitals in the U.S.A. during the first quarter of the year, following which the family moved to Paris. Near there, in the village of Clairfontaine, a house was found ("Le Pavillon") which became their summer home not only for 1929 but for several more years until the completion of the projected Swiss home, and where Rachmaninoff created around him anew the surroundings he had grown to love at Ivanovka in the past. At the end of this summer the past became present again with the news of the death of his mother, Lubov Rachmaninova, in Novgorod.

About this time the composer, whose opposition to broadcasting was lifelong, but who extended a grudging acceptance to the gramophone — on the whole successfully — made a number of fresh recordings, of which the most famous and deservedly successful was that of the ever-popular Second Concerto with Stokowski and the Philadelphia Orchestra. Of almost equal historical importance are those of the *Isle*, the orchestrated *Vocalise,* and the charming performance with Kreisler of Schubert's Duo in A, op. 162.

Following the pattern determined the previous year, the autumn of 1929 commenced with a European tour. After five very successful concerts in Holland 15 were scheduled for England, including London recitals on November 3rd and 24th and a performance of the Fourth Concerto under Albert Coates on November 18th when the unlucky work failed once again to make any deep effect. Concerts in Paris and Berlin flanked a dozen or so other continental appearances, after which it was again time to cross the Atlantic.

At the beginning of 1930, negotiations took place between the publishers and Respighi, with Rachmaninoff's enthusiastic approval, for the former to orchestrate a selection of the Etudes-Tableaux (opp. 39 no. 2; 33 no. 7; 39 nos. 7, 6 and 9), a scheme which was brought to a successful conclusion during the year. Meanwhile, Rachmaninoff was touring in Canada and the U.S.A., this season with a programme of music by Chopin and Liszt, of which the centrepoint was the former's B flat minor sonata, which was also recorded about this time. By April, the tour was finished and the family sailed again for France, where Clairfontaine was to be their summer retreat once more; a summer of particularly happy relaxation, from all accounts, with many friends around including of course the Medtners — but still no composition. A decision which was taken during this summer however concerned the preparation of a book of memoirs. Of several propositions considered, the one which finally developed was to be in the hands of Oskar von Riesemann, who was living in Switzerland on Lake Lucerne. A subsequent visit to the latter's home determined the Rachmaninoffs at last to buy a permanent new home for themselves in this same area: having purchased a site at Hertenstein, they prepared to build there and in anticipation named it after their own names — Villa SeNaR. The autumn of the year, following the new custom, was devoted to a tour of the Continent and England; during which the last few public performances of the Fourth Concerto in its first published version were given, after which it was withdrawn for revision which did not mature for over 10 years.

Returned to America for his annual tour there early in 1931, Rachmaninoff made one of his unusual errors of judgment in entering an area of controversy when he added his signature to a letter of protest published in New York against Tagore's support of Soviet achievements in the world of education. Shortly afterwards, a ban on the teaching and performance of his compositions throughout the Soviet Union was pronounced, a bitter blow to the composer who never thought of himself as belonging to any other land than that of Russia. Nevertheless, this year was at last to see original work once again. After the American tour was finished, the summer at Clairfontaine, brightened by a visit amongst others of Chaliapin, was the scene for Rachmaninoff's last solo piano work: the Variations (op. 42) "on a theme of Corelli" dedicated to Fritz Kreisler, thanks to whom doubtless the author's introduction to the theme is due, a theme in key and stepwise structure so like

55

that of the Third Concerto. Though as pianistic as ever, in several variations one can imagine the tones of the dedicatee's instrument, pizzicato and all. At the very end comes an exquisite page of coda, where the melody rises to an altitude and with an expression which irresistibly recall the song of the great violinist — yet surprisingly, beneath Rachmaninoff's fingers, on his eloquent Steinway, the illusion was perfected. Another work of this summer was the complete rewriting of the Second Sonata, now slightly cut and considerably thinned in texture whilst losing none of its power and vitality. The concert transcription of Rimsky's "Flight of the Bumble Bee" also dates from this time.

From "Le Pavillon", Rachmaninoff and his wife went to Switzerland to watch the progress of the Villa Senar, where they were able to stay in one of the outbuildings for several weeks, returning to Clairfontaine en route for the New World. The new Variations, a grateful and effective work of not excessive difficulty, were introduced at the first recital of the autumn tour, in Montreal in October 1931. Shortly after, the brilliant little *Oriental Sketch* dating from 1917 and the last days in Russia was first publicly performed by the composer, who thenceforward frequently included it in his programmes. This season also, the newly-orchestrated Etudes-Tableaux were introduced by Koussevitzky and taken up by other conductors for inclusion in more than one complete programme of Rachmaninoff's work.

In Spring 1932, the composer's tour brought him to London again, where on March 10th, after a superb performance of the Third Concerto under Sir Henry Wood, he was given the gold medal of the Royal Philharmonic Society. During the ensuing summer, while work on Senar and its surroundings progressed, though slowly, Rachmaninoff's younger daughter Tatiana married Boris Conus and settled with him in Paris. When the composer returned to America in October, his recital programme was an extended version of the "feature" programme of fantasies, now

56

including works by Haydn and Schumann and Scriabin's
Sonata—Fantasy as well as the works by Beethoven, Chopin
and Liszt named before. This season, his tour was somewhat extended to the south and west, and it was March
1933 before it finished on the eve of Rachmaninoff's six-
tieth birthday, the fortieth anniversary of his first appearance as a pianist having been marked by a short ceremony
in New York the previous December.

Celebrations continued in Paris, which was reached in
April, and the London recital on April 29th was the
occasion for introducting not only the "Corelli" variations
but also a new Bach transcription — the prelude from the E
major violin partita, later to be rounded off with the
Gavotte and Gigue — and the Mendelssohn Scherzo transcription. As an example of Rachmaninoff's recital programmes, and the last London one introducing a solo "first
performance" there, the whole details are now listed:—

Preludio from Violin Sonata in E major	— Bach (trans. S.R.)
Sonata in F minor, op. 57	— Beethoven
Nocturne in F sharp major Ballade in A flat major	— Chopin
Variations on a theme of Corelli, op. 42 Two Preludes, op. 32 (B minor, A minor)	— Rachmaninoff
Nachtstück, op. 23 no. 4	— Schumann
Invitation to the Dance	— Weber — Tausig
Scherzo from "A Midsummer-Night's Dream"	— Mendelssohn (trans. S.R)

57

After the conclusion of these concerts, Senar was the destination, and this year the purchase of a large speed-boat added exploration of the Lake (and races with the official steamers) to the somewhat less-expected pleasures of the grave concert artist. Receipt of the proofs for approval of von Riesemann's recently-finished book were an unpleasant surprise: the publisher's title "Rachmaninoff's Recollections" and the lengthy passages in simulated direct reportage very much upset the retiring composer, who insisted on considerable pruning, in particular of what he was credited with having said about his own work. This being completed to his agreement, if not his satisfaction, he provided an introductory letter of authorization and a few musical MSS. fragments in facsimile, and the book duly appeared the following year. During this 1933—4 concert season in the States, the welcome news was received that the Soviet ban on the composer's music had been lifted, and performances including the recent opp. 40, 41 and 42 were proceeding as before in his native land. London in March (10th), Paris in April, thus according to the regular pattern the tours continued relentlessly; but this April the Villa Senar was at last completed, and there Rachmaninoff and his wife arrived to find all in order and even a new piano installed as a gift from Steinways. Here too, as a proof of the value to him of this newly-constructed home, the composer again resumed work and produced the one absolutely unequivocal success of his later years: the Rhapsody on a theme of Paganini (op. 43) for piano and orchestra. In this score, the lighter texture of the Fourth Concerto plus a new whimsical touch, the Dies Irae motif and the intensely characteristic D flat melody based on the inversion of Paganini's theme (in variation 18) all combine into one brilliant and harmonious whole falling into a three-movement concerto outline despite its continuous and cumulative strict variation structure.

Returning to America, the new work was introduced in

Baltimore in November 1934 and played with a success throughout the remainder of the season which continued when the composer crossed to the Old World early in 1935 and reached a climax at the brilliant London premiere under Sir Thomas Beecham on March 21st that year. This return to successful large-scale composition, for which in form and content the solo Variations op. 42 had been a trial, undoubtedly rekindled the composer's enthusiasm; for during the summer vacation in Senar this same year, an even larger work was started: the Third Symphony in A minor (op. 44). Two of the three movements of which the work consists were finished this year, but the approach of another season of concerts and recitals deferred its completion until the next holiday. This time, the European wing of the tour extended farther East than ever before — to Warsaw, in fact — but back in Senar by June 1936 the new Symphony was resumed and carried to a successful conclusion. Meanwhile another important task had been carried out: the rewriting of the difficult chorus parts in the third movement of *The Bells,* of which Sir Henry Wood was to give the long-delayed Sheffield performance in October. Possibly because of the rewriting being largely concerned with the English words, this revision is completely overlooked by the Russian State publications of the work, although the latter give a careful comparison of the slightly differing vocal and full scores of the Gutheil edition. Much later even further (and presumably final) revisions came to light in the publisher's archives, possibly dating from the composer's own performances of this favourite work in the 1940s, and these were included in a choral score published by Boosey and Hawkes as recently as 1971.

Rachmaninoff performed the Rhapsody in London again in October 1936 on his way to Sheffield, where he gave the Second Concerto as well as assisting in the preparations for *The Bells,* before returning to America: the new Symphony was first played in Philadelphia on November 6th, performances in many other cities following. No repetition of the success of the Rhapsody greeted the new score either at its first or subsequent performances; first in Russia after the War did it become valued in its true perspective, as a concise and typical expression of the composer's later manner. Less expansively lyrical, perhaps, than the second symphony, in the long arches of melody which close the first and second movements and the gradual build-up in the coda to the third it is a worthy partner to its two predecessors.

1937 opened with *The Bells* performed on tour by Ormandy, and the composer again visiting the American mid— and far-West, before (in March) he crossed to England, thence to Paris and Senar. During this summer, visited by Michel Fokine, the first thoughts of collaboration in a ballet based on the Paganini story and utilizing the music of the Rhapsody were mooted and expanded by Rachmaninoff in a subsequent letter to the famous choreographer. Before returning to America, the composer revisited London in September to conduct a recording of the Third Symphony, which work was first publicly performed in England by Beecham the following November 18th. Between October and the end of the year, 32 American concerts took place, and in February 1938 an extensive European tour commenced, during which for the first time for many years Rachmaninoff played another composer's concerto — Beethoven's evergreen first. The London recital on March 12th. which opened with Liszt's "Weinen Klagen" prelude — and not the variations of the same title, for which the programme note had prepared the audience, — must in consequence have been one of the few occasions when Rachmaninoff's piano playing was received with absolute silence. The tour was to have ended in Vienna with the composer conducting *The Bells* and the new symphony; a concert cancelled by the march of military events. Meanwhile, the death of Chaliapin in Paris in April, where Rachmaninoff had daily visited him in hospital, broke one of the last and closest links with the earliest days of his musical career in Russia.

Revisions to the new symphony were in hand all this time, during which several successful performances had been given by Wood; including one at a Promenade concert devoted to Rachmaninoff's works, which also featured the prelude to the *Miserly Knight* and the orchestrated *Vocalise*. On October 5th 1938, at the Albert Hall, a special Henry Wood Jubilee Concert took place, at which the only foreign artist was Rachmaninoff himself, who came specially to play his Second Concerto. After the customary American season in the autumn, the composer visited the Old World for the last time in the spring of 1939. The English tour included two London recitals, the second of which on March 11th at least reached a height even Rachmaninoff had never surpassed in four Chopin Etudes (op. 25, nos. 7, 5, 4 and 12). Work was meanwhile proceeding apace on the new ballet, in which Dorati, who was to conduct, was associated with Fokine. Finally all was ready, and a brilliant success was scored at the first and all subsequent performances at Covent Garden (commencing on June 30th 1939). Outstanding from Paganini (—Rostoff)'s first entry, to the jerky skeleton of his own theme, many moments of new light were thrown on this now familiar score; such as that dazzlingly fast dance by the incomparable Riabouchinska to the F major variation (no. 15) accompanied by "Paganini" with equal virtuosity, now on his guitar; and the vision of the ineffably beautiful Baranova in the noble D flat variation.

Rachmaninoff, alas, was the only one unable to be present among these triumphs: he had slipped over on the polished floor at Senar and was bruised, shaken and so lame for many weeks that he was thus unable to witness his last great success, perhaps in an unexpected sphere, in London. International developments darkened this summer of 1939 all over Europe; but Rachmaninoff gave one final concert before returning for the last time to America: he played Beethoven's First Concerto and his own Rhapsody at the Lucerne Festival under Ansermet. His last exchange of letters with Wilshaw reveals the ever-increasing enthusiasm in Moscow for his recent compositions, and in return, Rachmaninoff outlines his plans for forthcoming seasons — onerous as they seem, it appears he feels stronger while he continues to take part in this chosen way of life. This American season commenced with a new venture — a performance of that Liszt work, the Totentanz, always beloved of Russian pianists and composers and a work which is one of the few progenitors of the Paganini Rhapsody. Next, the Philadelphia Orchestra under Ormandy gave a "Rachmaninoff Cycle" of concerts in New York to celebrate the thirtieth anniversary of the composer's first visit to the United States. Besides playing his first three concertos and the Rhapsody in programmes which also included the Second Symphony and the *Isle of the Dead* Rachmaninoff himself conducted the final programme of the Third Symphony and *The Bells;* thus giving a summing-up of his whole life's work.

By this time Europe was at War again; and Rachmaninoff was separated from his younger daughter in Paris, whom he never saw again, and his Swiss home so laboriously erected. But the restriction to America gave no reduction as yet in the strenuous nature of the concert tours: 41 appearances took place in the 1939 season, which extended for a welcome break to California. Early in 1940, several of the first piano pieces were reissued "revised and as played by the Composer", principally the Melody (op. 3 no. 3) wherein the original isometric chordal accompaniment was now dissolved into an elusive and almost improvisatory texture of haunting beauty. The famous Prelude, arranged by so many other hands into such various forms, had a little earlier been given an authentic two-piano setting by its author. Then, in the summer of 1940 spent at the "Orchard

Point" estate near Huntington, Long Island, the composer commenced his only original work to be entirely written in his adopted homeland of the U.S.A. — the Symphonic Dances (op. 45) which was also to be his last original score.

The composition of this work was shared with recital practice, just as the orchestration took place during the actual recital tours later in 1940, for the work was due to be first performed in Philadelphia in January 1941. Once again, an indifferent reception met this composition; the writing of which had however much pleased its author, who signed this score, like its predecessors, as did Haydn of old: "I thank thee, Lord". The section with the saxophone melody in the slow middle part of the first dance is as typical as any work of the composer's maturity, just as the lingering close of this movement recalls the parallel moment in *The Bells;* and the final bars of the whole work, through and after which the gong reverberates, resemble the end of the fateful symphony of 1895, as they close in the D minor with which the first orchestral work began over 50 years before.

During the later stages of the 1940—41 tour, Rachmaninoff again conducted *The Bells* and the Third Symphony, this time in Chicago; and when he settled in Huntington again for the summer it was to take up a long-promised task: the revision of the Fourth Concerto, op. 40. Further compression and tightening of the solo part in the second movement was followed by a fresh rewriting of the middle section of the finale and an entirely recomposed closing section, which maintained the taut momentum of the whole to an even surer conclusion. The only other work — the last one — of this summer was a piano transcription of Tchaikovsky's Lullaby, already transcribed by other hands including its own composer's. During the autumn concert tour this year besides the "new" Fourth Concerto (which was also then recorded) Rachmaninoff played, for the first time in America, the Schumann Concerto. Meanwhile, the composer's native land and his adopted homeland had both been attacked and so had both entered the War.

It was decided in 1942 that the Rachmaninoffs would spend this summer in California; and they first rented a house in Beverly Hills previous to purchasing the one on Elm Drive that was to be the composer's last home. After a summer of comparative relaxation there, darkened by the War news from everywhere, the absence of any word from his daughter Tatiana and the loss of several old friends, Rachmaninoff decided that his next tour, which would take him to his seventieth birthday, should be his last; after which he would retire to the beautiful climate and surroundings of his new and much-loved home and garden. A number of concerts for charities and War relief were given; and this last tour began in October, being planned to have a six-week rest around the turn of the year. At the last New York concert in December, the Symphonic Dances were given again, this time under Mitropolos, and the composer played his Rhapsody; followed by a party to celebrate the fiftieth anniversary of his first concert appearance.

Before the tour resumed, in February, it was clear that Rachmaninoff was far from well, losing weight and exhibiting a number of disturbing symptoms. For years, the weariness with which he was overcome when tours ended had increased, though the persistent neuralgia which only eased when he was actually on the stage had been partially arrested; but these signs were different. However, he managed to perform the Rhapsody (and the Beethoven First Concerto) in Chicago to his own high standard, but a week later in Knoxville (Tennessee) he gave his last recital — only refusing to cancel it because he had already once before disappointed his agent there. Cancelling concerts in Florida, he rested awhile in New Orleans. Here however he became worse, and all remaining fixtures were abandoned as Rachmaninoff travelled slowly and painfully to Los Angeles and hospital. After a few days there he was taken home to Elm

64

Drive, where his condition gradually deteriorated still further. Tests soon established that his complaint was a rare but rapid form of cancer, already far advanced and beyond any form of human aid or treatment. Birthday greetings arrived from the Soviet composers in the name of his native land, but by then Rachmaninoff was unconscious; and on March 28th 1943, four days before his seventieth birthday, he died in his own house barely six weeks after his last concert in a series lasting fifty years. His body was taken back to New York State and buried in Kensico Cemetery — near Valhalla.

It was Rachmaninoff's wish that at his funeral the fifth hymn of his Vespers should be sung; for various reasons this was not carried out — let its opening bars stand here, then, as his Nunc Dimittis.

"Lord, now lettest thou thy servant depart in peace"

Ex.(4): Night Vigil (Vespers), op. 37 no. 5, bars 1—6

CONCLUSION

We have now traced, albeit hurriedly at times, the links in the chain of Rachmaninoff's life and work. It is appropriate now to say a few words on the man himself, before listing his principal compositions in conclusion of our study.

In person Rachmaninoff was very tall and spare, soberly restrained in manner and garb and taciturn to a degree not to be explained away entirely in later years by his poor command of the English language. He always wore his hair cropped short, "like a convict" as Chaliapin said, and appeared on the stage "dressed like an undertaker" according to the same authority, who offered to teach him how he should bow to his audiences. At his ease perhaps above all with his family, and also in the congenial company of his fellow-countrymen, he was happiest in those surroundings which formed the background to the greater part of his mature creative life: the Russian landscape around Ivanovka, which he came to love even more than that around Borisovo and the Novgorod of his youth. A similar entourage he endeavoured to create in various places in America; with Clairfontaine and later Senar, especially the latter, supplying at different times his need for gardens, trees and crops. As a younger man he was an excellent horseman, a love of horses being inherited from his father. The motor car purchased after his initial American trip became the first of several at the controls of which, as of his speedboats, the concert performer found complete if surprising relaxation. (His pleasure in novel means of transport brought him across the Atlantic in the Graf Zeppelin one occasion in the 'thirties).

In his letters, now collected and published in Russia, we find often a vein of quiet humour which tempers the generally sardonic tone. But as we have insisted from our opening words, which quoted the composer himself, music was his life; and in the last resort it was as a superlative executant that for most of this life he found happiness in fulfilment. "I know only one thing," he said in a letter to his friend Wilshaw back in Russia, "that while working I somehow feel inwardly stronger than without work. Therefore may God grant me to work up to the last days." How this prayer was granted him, we have already seen.

At the keyboard, Rachmaninoff's manner was as utterly reserved as would be expected; not for him the theatrical gesture, on or off stage, in life or music. Once when lumbago made him unable to rise and leave the piano, he caused his assisted exit to be masked by the curtains: nothing extraneous must intrude on his music-making. And as Stravinsky, not always the kindest of critics, said, "he was the only pianist I have ever seen who did not grimace. That is a great deal." To him, piano-playing was not just another "accomplishment" but was the embodiment of the whole man — that whole man, we remember, being 85% musician. His utter conviction, complete control, formidable power and yet the clarity of the total texture allied to an unequalled rhythm and infinite variety of tone were approached only by Hofmann and Lhévinne amongst all his contemporaries. Ernest Newman, doyen of the London critics, once spoke of his piano playing as being so good that it made the best of what most other pianists could give sound merely second-rate; and Josef Hofmann himself wrote "even when you do not play as well as you are able to, your execution still bears the stamp of mastery." The same great artist, in a touching posthumous tribute, said: [He had] "steel in his arms, gold in his heart. I can never think of this majestic being without tears, for I not only admired him as a supreme artist but I also loved him as a man." The gifts which inspired these tributes were surely not the results of mere schooling alone. It is nevertheless clear that the rigorous discipline initiated under the Zverev regime laid the firm foundation on which it was later possible to build a career that ranged over New and Old Worlds for more than fifty years.

Some idea of the programmes offered by Rachmaninoff in his years as a virtuoso will have been gathered from the third part of our essay. Bach and Beethoven, Chopin and Liszt, Schumann, little Brahms and only early Debussy, one or two of his own works "for the sake of appearances", as he used to say: these formed the mainstay of his recitals in later years, with occasional items by Grieg, Scriabin, Borodin or Medtner to add variety. Few occasions failed to include the C sharp minor prelude among the generous encores!

This is not the place to attempt an assessment of Rachmaninoff's ultimate position in the musicians' Hall of Fame. Suffice it to say that, even though he may not be numbered amongst the select company of the giants — Bach, Mozart, Beethoven — nor included with the innovators such as Debussy, he has a secure niche beside Liszt's as both composer and the greatest pianist of his generation. As such, he enriched the repertoire of his instrument with two or three of the most deservedly-popular concertos, both with pianists and their audiences, then and after; besides leaving a mass of other music (much of it still less than well-known), of which it will be enough to recall the wealth of songs and those two great choral works, so different from each other: *The Bells* and the Vespers.

In his private life Rachmaninoff appears to have been exceptionally happy in his marriage, and devoted to his wife and their two daughters. "It's about *them* that a book should be written!" he once said to Wilshaw, shrugging aside Riesemann's book on himself; "I think to myself that evidently somewhere in my life I did one good deed, for which God sends me this joy," he wrote to the same friend on another occasion, speaking of his children.

Rachmaninoff was fortunate early to find a publisher

68

who, having assured his own position with popular publications, was prepared to invest in a young and then unknown name. Gutheil remained faithful to his protégé for years, in fact until the absorption of his firm into Koussevitzky's "Edition Russe" on his death. After settling in the U.S.A., most of Rachmaninoff's later compositions were first published by Carl Fischer, then by Charles Foley together with some issues from Paris over the imprint of TAIP (Tair), an anagram of the initial letters of his daughters' names. After the War, almost all the hitherto-unpublished completed juvenilia remaining in Russia were published there by the State Publishers, who also undertook a Collected Edition of the piano works edited by Pavel Lamm and later of the songs as well. Most of the other works were then reprinted and full scores were engraved and issued for the first time in some cases. The composer's characteristically accurate notation (and proof-reading) has the result that textual problems rarely arise in considering the original publications of his work.

The manuscripts of almost all of Rachmaninoff's works written before his flight from Russia appear to be in the Rachmaninoff room of the State Central (Glinka) Museum of Musical Culture in Moscow; those of his "American" works, together with the archival materials so carefully and devotedly collected and preserved by his wife and his sister-in-law Sophia Satina, are now in the Library of Congress, Washington D.C. A detailed listing of the published compositions, only needing minimal adjustments and updating, appears in the massive work, "Sergei Rachmaninoff" by S. Bertensson and J. Leyda (Allen & Unwin, 1965). Based as it is on the archive abovementioned, and enhanced by the personal assistance of Mme. Satina, that volume has been the principal authority (other than the printed music) consulted by the present compiler, who stands deeply indebted to those authors as need be all subsequent writers.

In conclusion, we now give a brief summary of Rachmaninoff's published principal compositions, arranged in categories, for the quick reference of students and other interested persons.

LIST OF PRINCIPAL COMPOSITIONS

(Most of the works up to op. 39 are generally available from Boosey and Hawkes Music Publishers Limited, the successors to the original publishers, Edition A. Gutheil and Edition Russe de Musique. A few exceptions, such as op. 16 (originally published by Jurgenson) are now handled by Richard Schauer. Of the late works, opp. 40 and 43 are available in the Eulenberg miniature score series, while the present owners of those works published by Charles Foley are now Belwin-Mills Inc. (Schott & Co. in U.K.). The posthumous early works, as already stated, are published by the Russian State Publishers, Moscow.)

Piano solo: Various early pieces (1887—91)

op.	3.	Five Morceaux de Fantaisie (1892) (Elegy; Prelude; Melody; Polichinelle; Serenade)
	10.	Seven Morceaux de Salon (1894) (Nocturne; Valse; Barcarolle; Melody; Humoresque; Romance; Mazurka)
	16.	Six Moments Musicaux (1896)
	22.	Variations on a theme by Chopin (1903)
	23.	Ten Preludes (1901—3)
	28.	Sonata no. 1 (D minor) (1907)
	32.	Thirteen Preludes (1910)
	33.	Eight Etudes — Tableaux (1911)
	36.	Sonata No. 2 (B flat minor) (1913, rev. 1931)
	39.	Nine Etudes — Tableaux (1916—17)

| | 42. | Variations on a theme by Corelli (1931) |
| | — | Oriental Sketch (1917) |

Piano duet:

| | op. 11. | Six pieces (Barcarolle; Scherzo; Russian Song; Valse; Romance; "Slava") (1894) |

Piano 6 hands:

| | — | Valse and Romance (1890—1) |

Two Pianos:

	—	Russian Rhapsody (1891)
	op. 5.	Fantaisie — Tableaux (Barcarolle; "O night, O love;" Tears; Easter) (1893)
	17.	Second Suite (Introduction; Valse; Romance; Tarantelle) (1900—1)

Chamber Music:

	—	Trio Elegiaque [no. 1] (G minor) (1892)
	2.	Two pieces for cello and piano (Prelude; Oriental Dance) (1892)
	6.	Two pieces for violin and piano (Romance; Hungarian Dance) (1893)
	9.	Trio Elegiaque [no. 2] (D minor) (1893)
	19.	Sonata for piano and cello (1901)

Piano and Orchestra:

| | op. 1. | First Concerto (F sharp minor) (1891, rev. 1917) |
| | 18. | Second Concerto (C minor) (1900—1) |

	30.	Third Concerto (D minor) (1909)
	40.	Fourth Concerto (G minor) (1926, rev. 1941)
	43.	Rhapsody on a theme of Paganini (1934)

Orchestra: Various early scores

	—	Prince Rostislav, poem (1891)
op.	7.	The Crag, fantasia (1893)
	12.	Capriccio on Gipsy Themes (1894)
	13.	First Symphony (D minor) (1895)
	27.	Second Symphony (E minor) (1906—7)
	29.	The Isle of the Dead, symphonic poem (1909)
	44.	Third Symphony (A minor) (1935—6)
	45.	Symphonic Dances (1940)

Songs: Various early songs (1890—1)

op.	4.	Six songs (1890—3)
op.	8.	Six songs (1893)
	14.	Twelve songs (1896)
	15.	Six choruses (1895)
	21.	Twelve songs (1900—2)
	26.	Fifteen songs (1906)
	34.	Fourteen songs (1910—12)
	38.	Six songs (1916)

Unaccompanied voices:

	—	Sacred concerto (1893)
	—	Pantelei, the Healer (A. Tolstoi) (1900)
op.	31.	Liturgy of St. John Chrysostom (1910)

37. Night Vigil (Vespers) (1915)

Voices and orchestra:
     op. 20.   Spring, cantata (1902)
        35.   The Bells, choral symphony (1913)
        41.   Three Russian Songs (1926)

Operas:
                Aleko (1892)
     op. 24.   The Miserly Knight (1903—4)
        25.   Francesca da Rimini (1900—5)

Arrangements for piano

of works by Bach, Bizet, Kreisler, Mendelssohn, Mussorgsky, Vasili Rachmaninoff, Sergei Rachmaninoff, Rimsky-Korsakov, Schubert, Tchaikovsky.